'No enemy plane will fly over the Reich territory'
Hermann Goering

'The bombers alone provide the means of victory'
Winston Churchill, 3 September 1940

'Moderation in war is imbecility'
Lord John Fisher, Admiral of the Fleet

THE AVRO
LANCASTER

WWII's most successful heavy bomber

Mike Lepine

© Danann Media Publishing Limited 2022

First Published Danann Publishing Ltd 2022

WARNING: For private domestic use only, any unauthorised Copying, hiring, lending or public performance of this book is illegal.

CAT NO: SON0515

Photography courtesy of

Getty images:

PhotoQuest	Popperfoto	Museum of Science and Industry, Chicago
Fox Photos	Imperial War Museum	The National Archives
Stringer	Science & Society Picture Library	PNA Rota
Hulton Deutsch / Hulton Archive	Mark Cuthbert	Harry Shepherd
Bettmann	Mirrorpix	
Central Press	Galerie Bilderwelt	

All other images, Wiki Commons

Cover design Darren Grice at Ctrl-d

Book layout & design Alex Young at Cre81ve

Tom O'Neill Copy Editor

All rights reserved. No Part of this title may be reproduced or transmitted in any material form (including photocopying or storing it in any medium by electronic means and whether or not transiently or incidentally to some other use of this publication) without the written permission of the copyright owner, except in accordance with the provisions of the Copyright, Designs and Patents Act 1988. Applications for the copyright owner's written permission should be addressed to the publisher.

Made in EU.
ISBN: 978-1-912918-79-9

ENTS

THE MANCHESTER	8
AVRO MANCHESTER	16
AVRO LANCASTER	28
1942	46
1943	72
1944	106
1945 AND BEYOND	122

THE MAN

One night Sir Arthur Harris, the Commander in Chief of Bomber Command, was speeding in his chauffeured, two-seater Bentley when he was stopped by the police. The policeman told him and his chauffeur that they could well kill someone driving like that. *'Young man,'* said Harris, *'I kill thousands of people every night.'*

THE BOMBER WILL ALWAYS GET THROUGH

In the early 1930s, the bomber was seen as little less than the harbinger of Armageddon. According to most tacticians, on the very first day of any future conflict the opposing nations would hurl their bomber fleets against each other's cities. Any fighter defences would simply be swatted away like insects as the bombers powered their way to their targets and unleashed pure hell in the form of high explosive and poison gas. Secret British government reports concluded that hundreds of thousands would die in the first few hours. The nation's hospitals would simply be overwhelmed by the maimed and the poisoned. Civilisation itself might fall.

And there was just no way to stop them. *'The Bomber will always get through'* was the maxim of the day. As Stanley Baldwin warned parliament in 1932:

'I think it as well for the man in the street to realize that there is no power on earth that prevents him from being bombed. Whatever people may tell him, the bomber will always get through…the only defence is offence, which means that you will have to kill more women and children more quickly than the enemy if you want to save yourselves.'

So it was a good thing that no-one was likely to use their bomber fleets in anger. They were a powerful deterrent. Their very existence assured the peace. The bombers didn't even have to be good. They just had to be there. This was fortunate for Britain. The pride of the Bomber Fleet, the Handley Page Heyford, introduced in 1933, struggled to fly at more than 100 mph. Other distinctly underwhelming types with which the British would wage any future war included the Fairey Battle, Bristol Blenheim, Handley Page Hampden, Vickers Wellesley, Armstrong-Whitworth Whitley and - the best of a bad bunch - the Vickers Wellington.

By 1936, it was increasingly looking like there *was* someone out there crazy enough to start a war. British Politicians realised that, compared with Nazi Germany, their bomber fleet was pitiful and its planes dangerously close to being outdated even before some could enter service. They needed bigger, better planes in a hurry.

SPECIFICATION P.13/36

In May 1936, Bomber Command was established. That same year, the British Air Ministry issued Specification P.13/36. They were looking for a major new twin-engined monoplane medium bomber. The specification was ambitious. The new bomber needed to be capable of deploying anywhere in the world and operating as a dive bomber or torpedo bomber as and when required. Its minimum speed needed to be 275mph at 15,000 and its bomb load 8,000lbs.

The eventual winners were announced in 1937 and the designs from Avro and Handley-Page were both selected. Shorts also elected to continue to develop their Stirling design.

The new Avro 679 was to be powered by two Rolls Royce Vulture engines. It would be 70 feet long with a wingspan just exceeding 90 feet and seven crew members. It was designed to be both easy to manufacture and to repair. To increase the size of the bomb bay, fuel tanks would be located within the wings. Protection would be provided by three gun turrets in the nose, mid-upper and rear positions. A ventral or belly turret was considered for later marks but never happened. The turrets offered a total of eight .303 machine guns - two in the nose, two in the dorsal turret and four in the rear turret. Its maximum bomb load would be 10,350 lbs.

LEFT: Air Marshal Sir Arthur Harris

ROY CHADWICK

The mind behind the Manchester was Roy Chadwick. Born in 1893, Chadwick came from a long line of Lancastrian engineers. As a boy he constructed ambitious model aircraft made in part from his mother's purloined silk blouses - but only flew them at night in a field behind his house because he was afraid people would laugh at him. He joined A.V. Roe & Company in 1911 as Roe's personal assistant, aged 18, and went on to create most of Avro's designs up to and including the earliest concepts of the Vulcan V-Bomber, for which he created the famous Delta Wing design over Christmas 1946/47. In total, Chadwick designed some 200 aircraft, 35 of which became production models.

ABOVE: A portrait of Chadwick with an Avro Lancaster and the Avro logo is displayed in the Renold Building at the University of Manchester

THE AVRO 679 MANCHESTER

Avro's new aircraft was expected to replace Britain's older bombers by 1939, but almost from the start, the Manchester failed to live up to its promise. The prototype, L7246, was principally designed by Avro's chief designer Roy Chadwick, put together by Avro's Experimental Department at Manchester's Ringway Airport and was first test flown there for 17 minutes on 25 July 1939. The test pilot admitted it was *'a bit of a handful'*. A later test flight on 30 August concluded that the Manchester was *'not at all satisfactory'*. Its performance proved far poorer than expected, mainly due to its Rolls-Royce Vulture engines which had promised real power and then failed to deliver. To make matters worse, Vulture engines also proved to be both temperamental and unreliable. Some were so poorly constructed that oil circulation problems would affect the bearings causing the piston to shear off and destroy the entire engine. Vultures ran hot and demanded constant attention from the pilot. In other incidents, a Vulture engine might just catch fire for no discernible reason. There were also wider problems with the airframe design and construction.

Because of the failings of the Vultures, the Manchester truly struggled ever to reach its intended operational ceiling of 19,200 feet. Instead, with a full bomb load it could barely reach 10,000 feet and strained to reach that. However, so desperate were the Air Ministry for the aircraft that they had started placing firm orders before the first prototype had even taken to the air. 200 were ordered in early July 1937, and a further 200 shortly thereafter.

BELOW: A Royal Air Force flight crew walks from their Avro 679 Manchester bomber. The aircraft is in service with the Royal Air Force Bomber Command

WAR

None of the new generation of bombers were ready for service when war broke out in 1939. The first Stirling flew in May 1939, but unfortunately crashed and did not join RAF service until August 1940. The HP56 prototype finally flew in October 1939 and the first aircraft - now called the Halifax - were supplied to No.35 Squadron in November 1940. Bomber Command would have to fly largely obsolete aircraft into action, still hoping that '*the bomber will always get through.*' As it was, neither Hitler nor Chamberlain unleashed their fleets as had been predicted. Instead they waited.

In the earliest months of the war, RAF Bomber Command's 536 aircraft operated under the very strictest of rules. The private property of Germans was not to be damaged under pain of criminal responsibility (this included military factories) and no civilians were to be hurt under any circumstances. To complicate matters further, neither the French nor Belgians would allow British bombers to fly through their airspace, in case it upset the Germans. This rather limited the sort of missions RAF Bomber Command could fly and the early 'raids' were usually against German naval vessels at sea or night runs to drop propaganda leaflets on German cities. The Germans were said to be grateful for the extra toilet paper.

On 4 September 1939 - the second day of World War Two - Bomber Command launched their first attack of the war. Ten Blenheims and nine Wellingtons were sent after ships of the German navy in the Heligoland Bight. Half the Blenheims never came back and two of the nine Wellingtons were also destroyed. Among the crews there were just three survivors. On 29 September, a flight of five Handley-Page Hampdens were all shot down by Bf.109s. On 18 December, 12 out of 22 Wellingtons were shot down

BELOW: Wellington Mark X HE239 of No.428 Sqn. RCAF. It completed its bomb run despite losing the rear gunner and turret and then flew back home for a successful landing with its bomb bay doors stuck open due to lack of hydraulic power

RIGHT: People in London look at a map illustrating how the RAF is striking back at Germany during 1940

by a force of 44 German Bf.109s and Bf.110 interceptors in just 20 minutes. It was becoming increasingly obvious that bombers in daylight were almost helpless against enemy fighters. During the Blitzkrieg in France in May-June 1940, even with the best fighter escort, it was typical of Blenheims to suffer an average loss of 25% during a raid. Fairey Battles fared even worse, and it was not unusual for 50% to be lost on a single mission. On some stations, crews were being killed before they could even unpack.

Daylight raids were turning into massacres, so Bomber Command largely switched to bombing under the cover of darkness. Now they found a new problem. On 15/16 May 1940, a strong RAF bomber force set off to do their own blitzing of the Ruhr, Germany's industrial heartland. Three quarters of them couldn't find it. More and more night raids on the Ruhr followed, targeting air fields, steelworks and oil refineries. Losses were high and results negligible. Night bombers couldn't navigate with sufficient accuracy to even find their targets, let alone hit them, even under ideal conditions. On 27 May 1940, a bomber from 10 Squadron became so lost - having mistaken the Thames Estuary for the Rhine - that it accidentally bombed an RAF fighter station at Bassingbourn in Cambridgeshire. Crews tried complex mathematics to find targets. They missed. Other crews tried flying low below cloud cover. They got killed.

The stakes kept getting raised. After a German bomber accidentally bombed London on 24 August 1940, Churchill ordered the bombing of Berlin. Out of 81 aircraft sent, only 29 actually found the third biggest city in the world. Just eight Germans died. In retaliation, 400 Luftwaffe aircraft bombed Coventry. In retaliation for this, in December 1940, 134 Bomber Command aircraft targeted Mannheim (to negligible effect). The press spoke for the British people when they demanded greater and greater revenge for the Blitz. They didn't care about German civilians being killed. There were already too many British dead. Bomber Command kept on trying to hit precision targets by night. And they kept on missing, unbeknownst to the general public. Results were so poor that German intelligence was quite baffled as to what the British were trying to achieve.

Churchill meanwhile was growing increasingly enthusiastic about the bomber offensive. It was, after all, pretty much all that Britain could throw at the Germans. He wanted more resources devoted to it. More planes, more raids. Better planes. Better technology. At the same time though, he was becoming increasingly suspicious of the glowing reports the RAF were giving him.

THE MANCHESTER

13

BELOW: The crew of a No 207 Squadron Royal Air Force Bomber Command Avro Manchester Mk.IA twin-engined medium bomber EM-O (L7483) prepare to board their aircraft for a mission circa October 1941 from their base at RAF Waddington near Lincoln, United Kingdom

THE MANCHESTER DELIVERED

The first production Avro Manchester, L7276, was delivered to the RAF on 5 August 1940, during the Battle of Britain. The first unit to be equipped with Manchesters was 207 Squadron, flying from RAF Waddington. They received their first aircraft in November 1940. 49, 50, 57, 61, 83, 97, 106, 408 and 420 Squadrons were all then equipped with Manchesters while a further few flew with Coastal Command.

TOP RIGHT: Orthographic projection of the Avro Manchester Mk I

RIGHT: Observer Corps aircraft spotter on the roof of a building in London during the Battle of Britain, with St. Paul's Cathedral in the background

CHESTER

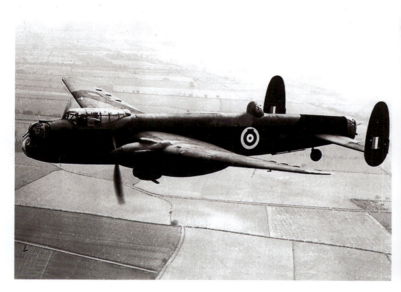

ABOVE LEFT: Avro Manchester Mk.1A 'L7486' (note extended tail fins)

ABOVE RIGHT: Interior view of a Manchester MK I

In truth, the Avro Manchester had been virtually written off by Bomber Command even before it saw active service. There were just too many problems with the design and they were not getting solved. This was realised by Roy Chadwick as early as mid-1940, when he began thinking about a massive reworking for the Manchester that would ditch the Vulture engines and instead feature four of the less powerful but promising new Rolls-Royce Merlin engines. This became referred to as the Type 683 Manchester III. The first prototype, BT308, flew from RAF Ringway, Cheshire, on 9 January 1941. Essentially it was an existing Mk.1 Manchester converted for use with four Merlins. Watching it, Avro's Managing Director Roy Dobson cried, *'oh boy, oh boy, what an aircraft!'*

THE MANCHESTER AT WAR

207 Squadron first flew the Manchester into combat on 24/25 February 1941, with six bombers attacking a German cruiser in Brest harbour. None were lost over the target, but one did crash on its way home due to mechanical problems. Less than a month later 207 lost their first Manchester, L7319, to enemy fire.

On 13 April 1941 all Manchesters were grounded due to high levels of engine failure. Despite desperate attempts to solve the problems with the Vultures, all Manchesters were grounded yet again on 16 June 1941. The faults with the Manchester were by now starting to affect the war effort. Bomber Command were forced to rely upon the obsolete Handley Page Hampden and sometimes could not scrape up enough aircraft of any type to launch a raid in good strength.

On 7 November 1941, Bomber Command launched a 400 aircraft raid on Berlin. Despite the Manchester being operated by eight Squadrons, only 15 were airworthy enough to take part. All Manchester production was finally shut down in November 1941 - but because of the war,

THE AVRO LANCASTER WWII'S MOST SUCCESSFUL HEAVY BOMBER

BELOW: Carrying Out Maintenance Work on an Avro Manchester Bomber, ca. 1941

existing aircraft were too valuable to scrap and instead they limped on. On 3 March 1942, just 35 Manchesters were able to take part in the first 1,000 bomber raid against Cologne. On 25 June 1942, Manchesters flew their last combat mission - against Bremen - They were then withdrawn and survivors used for training.

193 Manchesters were built in all. Of those, 177 were built by Avro and a further 32 by Vickers. A further 12 - the first off the production line - were destroyed by a Luftwaffe bombing raid just before Christmas 1940 and were not counted as delivered. 78 were lost to enemy action. A shocking 45 were lost to mechanical failures - 30 of which were due to problems with the Vulture engines. They flew some 1,269 sorties and dropped a total of 1,826 tons of bombs.

BELOW: The forward section of a Manchester Mark I at Waddington, Lincolnshire, showing the nose with the bomb-aimer's window, the forward gun-turret and the cockpit, September 1941

THE MANCHESTER MK III

Despite the overwhelming success of the new Manchester designs with four Merlin engines, no-one could muster any enthusiasm for another generation of Manchesters. So they called the aircraft the Lancaster instead.

Disregarding the change in engines, the Lancaster was in so many ways the same plane as the Manchester. Partially-constructed Manchesters on the assembly line were converted into what were designated as B.1 Lancasters. In wartime and with a real shortage of resources, this was a huge boost to Bomber Command. It meant they could get their much-anticipated Lancasters flying and fighting far faster. Along the way, the old Merlins were dropped in favour of Merlin XX engines and the first Lancaster to come off the production line first flew in November 1941.

ABOVE: A Rolls-Royce Merlin engine

THE BUTT REPORT

Initially no-one knew how effective or ineffective British bombing was. Bomber crew accounts tended to be on the 'excited side'. From 1941 onwards, cameras were fitted to bombers, triggered by the bomb release, to ascertain the true damage being done.

These photographs were used as the basis of what became known as The Butt Report. Initiated by Lord Cherwell and run by David Miles Bensusan-Butt, an economist at the Admiralty, the report looked at 633 photos taken of sites bombed. The final report, issued on 18 August 1941 provided a terrible shock at the very highest levels of government.

Each week, the Cabinet had been receiving a report from Bomber Command about the progress of the bombing.

The report for July 17-24, 1941, for example, told them that *'Over 670 tons of H.e. and over 58,000 incendiary bombs were dropped, and it is estimated that a large proportion of these fell in the target areas.'*

The truth was actually very different.

Of the aircraft which reported hitting their target, only one in three on average got anywhere near five miles of their target. The actual figure varied with the target area. Over the French Ports - relatively easy targets - two in three bombers attacked the right area. Over Germany as a whole that figure fell to one in four and - over the Ruhr with its heavy defences - numbers fell to one in ten. On nights with no moon to fly by, only 1 in 15 bombers came within five miles of their target. 49% of all bombs dropped

THE AVRO LANCASTER WWII'S MOST SUCCESSFUL HEAVY BOMBER

22

BELOW: An Avro Manchester Mk1A twin-engine heavy bomber L7427 OL- Q of No.83 Squadron Royal Air Force Bomber Command flying on 21 April 1942 near Scampton, United Kingdom

were falling on open countryside. Someone joked that far more cows were being killed than Germans.

Given further considerations like being deflected by night fighters, mechanical problems and bad weather, the final estimate was that only 5% of all bombers despatched ever got within five miles of their target. What's more it had been estimated elsewhere that up to 40% of British bombs would fail to explode, no matter where they dropped. A further report estimated that, to kill just one German on the ground, the RAF would have to drop 5 tons of bombs. They were losing one bomber for every ten tons. *'This is a very serious paper and seems to require urgent attention,'* commented Churchill.

By the end of 1941, Bomber Command was experiencing such heavy losses - and hitting so few targets to any effect - that the whole bomber effort was being called in question and missions began to decrease significantly. There was

ABOVE: Interior of RAF Fighter Command's Sector 'G' Operations Room at Duxford, Cambridgeshire, September 1940

RIGHT: The flight crew of an Avro Manchester Mk 1A of No.207 Squadron Royal Air Force Bomber Command line up beneath the aircrafts forward section showing the nose with the bomb-aimer's window, the forward gun-turret with twin .303 Browning machine guns and the pilot's cockpit before an operation on 12 September 1941 at RAF Waddington, United Kingdom

even talk of shutting it down and sharing out its resources between the army and the navy.

Given the undisputable fact that there was no way that Bomber Command could hit a precision target by day or night, Lord Cherwell produced a 'Dehousing Document'

in March 1942, suggesting that area bombing (i.e. hitting a very large target, for example a city) could be the way forward. The target would be the homes of German workers involved in industries vital to the German war effort. His suggestion was enthusiastically embraced by

The Secretary of State for Air, Sir Archibald Sinclair, and Chief of the Air Staff Sir Charles Portal since they could not see how else to solve the problems Bomber Command was experiencing.

LEFT:
RAF recruitment posters

DESIGN AND BUILD

The first Lancasters to see operational use were just a shade under 70 feet long, with a wingspan of 102 feet. Empty, they weighed 36,900 lb and their maximum take-off weight was set at 68,000 lb. Fully laden, they were capable of speeds up to 282 mph at 13,000 feet when required, but average cruising speed was closer to 200 mph. Maximum altitude was 21,400 feet fully laden. Their range was just over 2,000 miles.

The first government contract for Lancasters specified 1,070 aircraft. Most would be built at the Avro factory at Chadderton near Oldham, Greater Manchester. Demand would soon exceed the capability of just one factory and so the Lancaster Aircraft Group was set up to allow other manufacturers to produce the aircraft. Metropolitan-Vickers

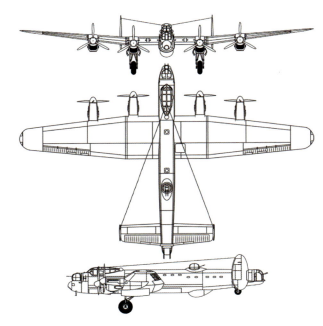

alone built 1,080 aircraft. Other contributors included Armstrong Whitworth and the Austin Motor Company at Longbridge in Birmingham.

A Lancaster in 1942 would cost just under £42,000 to build. It also took over 70,000 man hours to assemble, with more than 55,000 parts - not including nuts, bolts etc. The process took 10 weeks.

ABOVE: Line drawing of Lancaster B Mk1

LEFT: Avro Lancaster aircraft under construction at the A V Roe & Co Ltd factory at Woodford in Cheshire, 1943

OPP. PAGE TOP: Workers sit inside the cockpit of an aircraft as they wire up the pilot's instrument panel, at a factory somewhere in Britain

OPP. PAGE BOTTOM: Avro Lancaster bombers nearing completion at the A V Roe & Co Ltd factory at Woodford in Cheshire, 1943

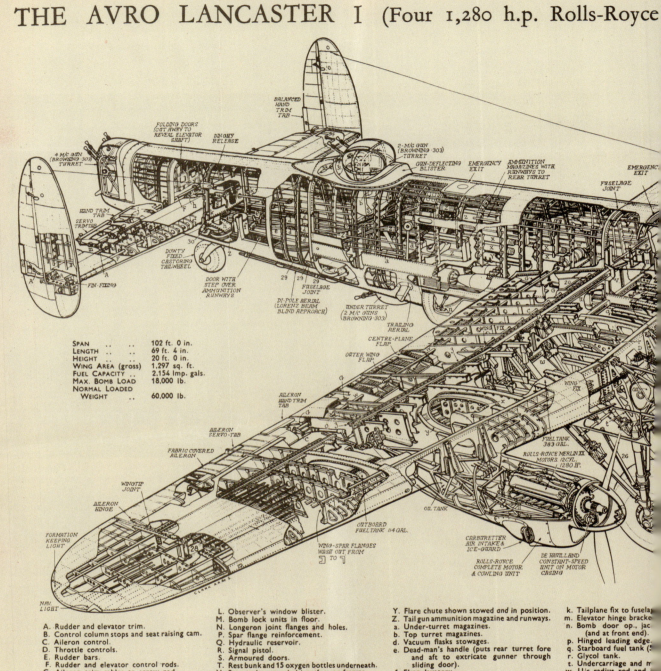

(...lin XX Motors)

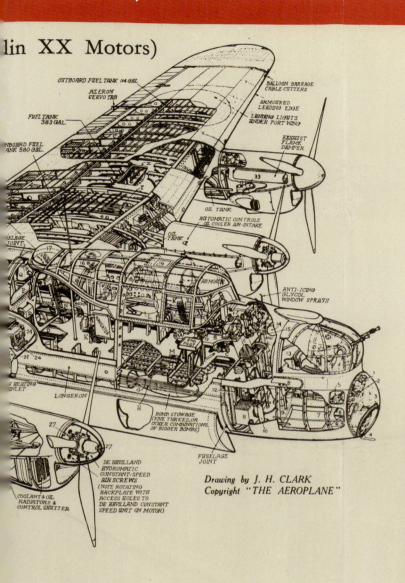

Drawing by J. H. CLARK
Copyright "THE AEROPLANE"

This is what YOU are making ...

Maximum Speed .... 300 m.p.h.
" Range .... 3000 miles.
FOUR GUN TURRETS
10 BROWNING ·303 s.

y. Fuel tank support strap.
z. Wing trailing section spar (bolted to wing rear spar).
1. Navigation light.
2. Bomb aiming sight.
3. Flat window (no distortion) and glycol anti-icing spray pipe.
4. Air-speed pressure head.
5. Glycol pump for "3."
6. Bomb aimer's body rest.
7. Emergency exit.
8. Ventilator.
9. Camera (through floor).
10. Pump.
11. Glycol tank (window spray) and step.
12. Bomb aimer's squint into bomb bay.
13. Detail of front turret mounting ring.
14. Compressed air bottle.
15. Pilot's glycol pump (cockpit window spray).
16. D.F. loop.
17. Astro-dome.
18. Rubber headroom buffer (cut away to show half-framed jointing). Note bullet-proof glass panel above.
19. Curtain.
20. Dinghy stowage (starboard wing).
21. Radiator control jack and rods.
22. Fuel cocks (remote controlled).
23. Hot glycol pipes into cabin heater.
24. Worm drive (cabin air heat controls) and air overflow.
25. Service pipes along leading edge.
26. U/c door op. link rod.
27. Spinner and back plate fixing to airscrew hub.
28. Wing-tip joint.
29. Downwards identification lamps.
30. Tailwheel leg hinge.
31. Taboo track and rollers.
32. Aerial spring suspension.
33. Carburetter air intake junction (up to carburetter).

MINISTRY OF AIRCRAFT PRODUCTION.
MALBY & SONS

RITISH WORKMANSHIP

CREW

Like the Manchester, the Lancaster had a crew of seven. The pilot sat within the greenhouse type canopy behind bulletproof glass on the port side of the aircraft. It is often thought that the pilot had a co-pilot but this was not true. The Lancaster was flown by a single individual, not least because it halved the need for trained pilots. Sitting beside him in the 'dicky seat' was the flight engineer, and behind them the navigator with his chart table and a bank of instruments showing things like airspeed which provided him with the information to (hopefully) work out where the aircraft was. His job was once compared to 'taking a seven hour maths exam while people tried to kill you.' Beside him, facing backwards down the aircraft was the wireless operator, who sat by the forward heater and controlled it. Positioned forward in the nose section was the bomb aimer, lying prone with the bombsight or else standing up to operate the forward guns. The crew was completed by a mid-upper gunner and a rear gunner.

MAIN IMAGE: The crew of a Lancaster bomber walk away from their plane after a flight while ground crew check it over

RIGHT TOP: Sergeant H H Turkentine, the bomb aimer on board an Avro Lancaster B Mark I of No. 57 Squadron RAF, at his position in the nose of the aircraft.

RIGHT MIDDLE: Flying Officer J B Burnside, the flight engineer on board an Avro Lancaster B Mark III of No. 619 Squadron RAF based at Coningsby, Lincolnshire, checks settings on the control panel from his seat in the cockpit

RIGHT BOTTOM: Flying Officer P Ingleby, the navigator of an Avro Lancaster B Mark III of No. 619 Squadron RAF based at Coningsby, Lincolnshire, seated at his table in the aircraft

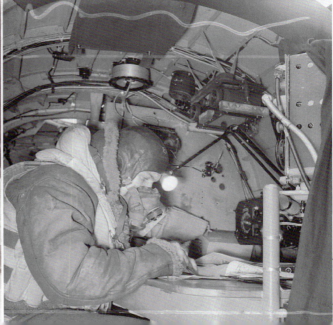

LIVING CONDITIONS

Cramped and uncomfortable was how most Lancaster crews would have described the interior. The Lancaster was not pressurised and crews needed a regular supply of oxygen. Towards the rear, temperatures could be cold as minus 40 in flight. Frostbite was common. Crew regularly lost fingers. The gunners were given heated suits to help them survive conditions and from 1944 ducts from the engines funnelled heat into their turrets. Relief in flight was provided by a chemical toilet situated close to the rear turret. Crewmen brave enough to use it found their buttocks freezing to the toilet seat and getting skinned.

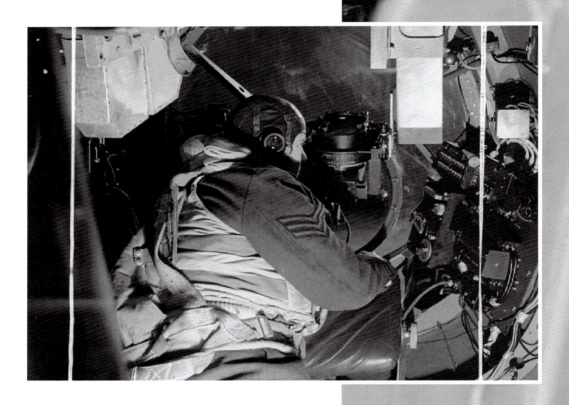

INSET: The bomb aimer in an Avro Lancaster, checking over the instruments in his position before take off from Scampton, Lincolnshire

MAIN IMAGE: Sergeant J B Mallett, a flight engineer on board an Avro Lancaster B Mark I of No. 57 Squadron at RAF Scampton, Lincolnshire, checks the readings on the aircraft's control panel

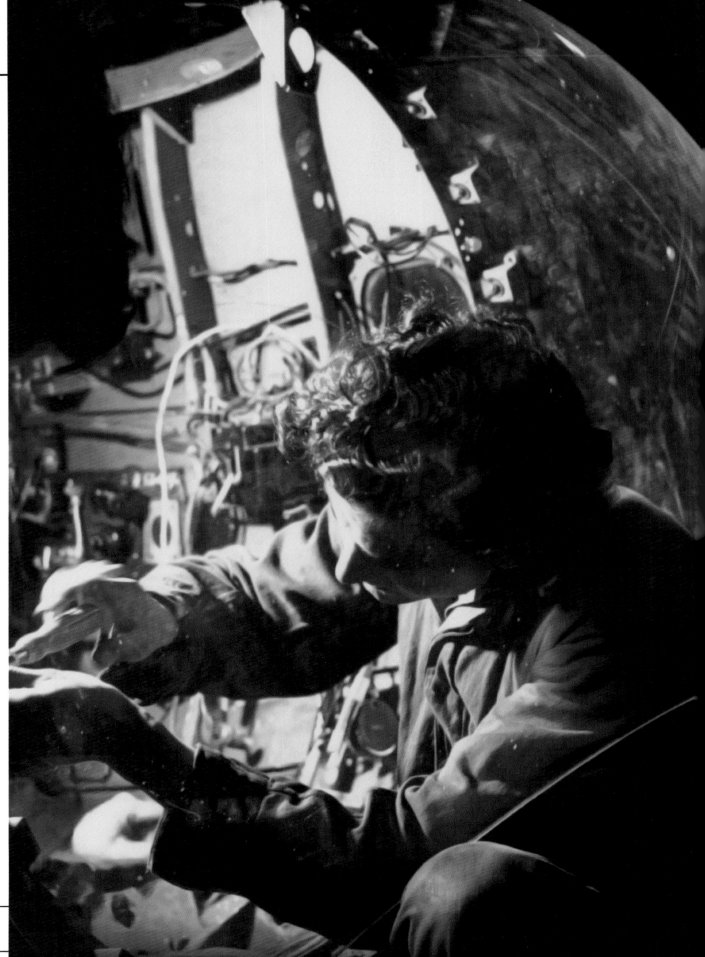

ESCAPE AND SURVIVAL

The Lancaster was sturdy and so able to absorb considerable battle damage. However in the first year of operation, pilots had to learn to respect its performance limitations. A number were lost early on after succumbing to structural failure when these limits were severely exceeded. Despite this, the Lancaster was known to be able to both loop and barrel roll and survive, something definitely not included in pilot training.

The rear turret was so small that rear gunners would usually not attempt to squeeze inside with their parachute on. Instead, they'd hang it off a hook further back in the fuselage and hope they could reach it if needed. Having seized their parachutes and strapped them on, they would then rotate their turrets until the outside was exposed and they could simply fall out. That was the theory.

In an emergency, there were two exits. The largest was the side crew door near the rear of the fuselage, but this was notoriously difficult for crew members seated forward because the way to it was obstructed by very large spars for the wings. It was also dangerous to use, as having jumped, the crewman could be snatched up by the slipstream and hurled against the tail plane.

A hatch lay underneath the bomber aimer's position but - being just 22in x 26.5in in size - it proved exceedingly difficult for an airman with a parachute to squeeze through. This problem was recognised and attempts were made to improve the Lancaster's hatch over the course of the war, but for whatever reason this never happened. There was also the risk of being sucked into one of the propellers once out.

Just 15% of Lancaster aircrew managed to successfully bail out of a stricken aircraft during the war. American crews on B-17s with larger escape hatches, by comparison, managed to safely bail out 50% of the time. Even Halifax crews had a 25% chance to jump.

ABOVE: Pilot officer E.T. Jones (left) of Edmonton, Alberta, and his navigator, flying officer E.N. Hooke, of Toronto, can stand practically any place in their Lancaster bomber "C for Charlie" and still have a view of the outdoors. Jones brought the battered ship back from his eleventh mission over Berlin with one engine out of action and heavy damage done to the starboard mainplane, bomb sides of the fuselage, rear turret, and controls

MAIN IMAGE: Repairs being made to the nose section of an Avro Lancaster heavy bomber at a Ministry of Aircraft factory after being damaged during raids on Berlin

TURRET GUNS

The Lancaster started out with four protective gun positions, nose, mid upper, rear and ventral (underside). However it was soon discovered that crews found the ventral guns awkward and slow to use and they were discontinued.

The front guns were fired by the bomb aimer and consisted of two .303 machine guns. The mid-upper gunner was tasked with defending both the rear and the sides of the aircraft. Lancasters started off with FN (Frazer Nash) 50 turrets sporting two .303 Brownings and mainly replaced them later on in the war with FN 150s, which offered better gunsights and more responsive controls. Both had an interrupter device to stop an over-excited gunner from blowing away his own tail fins. Other types of turret were experimented with and the last of the Lancaster X's ended up sporting Martin 250 CE 23A turrets with electrical controls and two .50 calibre guns. The rear gun turret started out as an FN 20 type with four .303 machine guns, but crew felt that the FN 20 was not as good as it could be and numerous types and modifications were attempted. The FN 20 was eventually replaced by the FN 120 which had an improved gyroscopic gun sight. The rear gunner typically carried 2,500 rounds per gun out on a mission, and to stop the ammunition from unbalancing the plane, it was stored underneath the mid-upper gunner's position and fed back down the aircraft to the rear turret.

In 1944 the FN-121 Automatic Gun Laying turret appeared, complete with 'Village Inn' gun-laying radar. The combining of guns with radar proved far more deadly, and Lancasters fitted with this used to deliberately hang around at the rear of a formation, pretending to be damaged stragglers. Expecting easy prey, German fighter pilots would concentrate on them and quickly find themselves on the receiving end of withering and highly accurate fire. Operational losses fell considerably.

OPP. PAGE: The rear gunner of a Lancaster of No. 44 Squadron peeks out through a cut-out in the perspex of his gun turret, October 1942

ABOVE: Nose turret guns of an Avro Lancaster B Mark X

BELOW LEFT: Avro Lancaster Mk X bomber, dorsal twin .50 Browning gun turret

BELOW LEFT: Rod cleaning the front machine guns of Avro Lancaster R5666/'KM-F', while another member of the ground crew cleans the cockpit window

AVRO LANCASTER

RIGHT: World War II Vintage 1940's Propaganda Poster. The Attack Begins In The Factory, 1943, by Artist Roy A. Nockolds

ABOVE: Post Office Savings Bank poster 1943 designed by Tom Eckersley

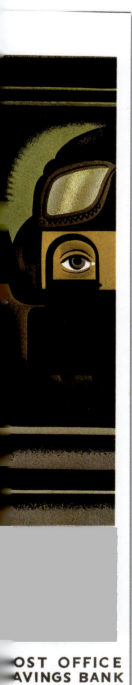

The big raids on Germany continue. British war plants share with the R.A.F. credit for these giant operations.

THE ATTACK BEGINS IN THE FACTORY

BOMB TYPES

The Lancaster inherited from the Manchester a superb 33ft long bomb bay, the largest then in use. Its bombload was fully twice that of the B-17. The first missions dropped mainly 4,000 lb HC (High Capacity) Cookies' or 'Dangerous Dustbins'. However, 305 of Lancaster Bs were fitted with bulged doors which enabled them to upgrade to carrying 8,000lb ordnance. To take the 12,000lb 'Tallboy' and 22,000lb 'Grand Slam' bombs, more modifications had to be made. Tallboys just required some work to the spars, but a Lancaster capable of carrying a 'Grand Slam' earthquake bomb had its dorsal turret removed as well as two of the four guns from the rear turret. Later versions also had the nose gun taken out. Strengthened versions of the undercarriage were applied and Merlin Mk 24 engines fitted to assist with take-off. The bomb bay doors were completely removed. Lancasters adapted to carry the Tallboy and Grand Slam were designated as Lancaster B.I or B.III Specials. Lancasters could also carry a variety of General Purpose High Explosive (GP/HE) bombs, incendiaries, armour-piercing weaponry, mines and depth charges.

BOTTOM LEFT TO RIGHT:
4,000 lb HC (High Capacity) Cookie; A 12,000-lb MC deep-penetration bomb, Bomber Command executive codeword 'Tallboy'; British 22,000 lb Grand Slam bomb; Flight Lieutenant P Walmsley, the bomb-aimer on board an Avro Lancaster B Mark III of No. 619 Squadron RAF, operating a Mark XIV Stabilised Vector Bombsight at his position in the nose of the aircraft

MAIN IMAGE: Bomb bay of a Lancaster

VARIANTS

Original versions of the Lancaster were designated the B.I and stayed in production until early 1946. The B.IIs were built exclusively by Armstrong Whitworth and were fitted with Bristol Hercules VI or XVI engines. Some 300 were manufactured. To confuse matters somewhat, the B.III was constructed at the same time as the B.I. and before the B.II. The B.II was conceived as a stop gap, allowing Hercules engines to be fitted when Merlins were in short supply. The only notable difference was the use of Packard Merlin engines (built in America) on the B.III. Virtually all British B.III's were manufactured at Avro's Newton Heath factory. The B.III was also manufactured in Canada by Victory Aircraft in Malton, Ontario, and was distinguished by being designated the B.X. It featured American-made electrics and instruments, and later a Martin dorsal turret in place of the Frazer Nash.

The B.IV was larger than the previous versions. Both the wingspan and the fuselage were enlarged. A new Boulton Paul F turret was also introduced, with two .303 Browning machine guns. This aircraft type became the Lincoln B.1. The B.V, which saw further enlarging of the wingspan and fuselage, was later designated the Lincoln B .2.

Only nine B.VI's is were built. They were essentially B.III's fitted with Merlin 85/87 engines designed to give all-round better performance, especially at high altitude. They were assigned exclusively to Pathfinder squadrons. Problems with the new engines saw the B.VI's all withdrawn from operations in November 1944.

The B.VII was the last version of the Lancaster to go into production. Noteworthy features included a Nash & Thomson FN-82 tail turret with twin 0.50 Browning machine guns and a Martin dorsal turret armed with two 0.5-inch Browning Mark II machine guns. Two different versions were made, one for use in Europe and the other for use in tropical climates, in anticipation of Lancasters being used in the Far East conflict as part of 'Tiger Force'.

RIGHT - CLOCKWISE FROM TOP LEFT:
MK I; MK I Special; MK II; MKiii

MAIN IMAGE:
Newly-completed Avro Lancaster B Mark IIIs on the apron of the A V Roe & Co. factory at Woodford, Cheshire

Photo reconnaissance versions were designated PR.I.'s. Flown by No. 82 and No. 541 Squadrons, they had all their weaponry and armour removed and a camera placed in the bomb bay. Other variants of note include the ASR.III/ASR.3, which was adapted for air-sea rescue roles and which carried a lifeboat in the bomb bay, and the GR.3/MR.3 which was a B.III adapted for maritime reconnaissance.

As well as giving rise to the Lincoln bomber, the Lancaster would evolve into the York transport, Lancastrian and Tudor airliners and the hugely successful Shackleton maritime patrol aircraft.

1942

'The Nazis entered this war under the rather childish delusion that they were going to bomb everyone else, and nobody was going to bomb them. At Rotterdam, London, Warsaw and half a hundred other places, they put their rather naive theory into operation. They sowed the wind, and now they are going to reap the whirlwind.'

Arthur Harris

'Bert Harris was the sort of buccaneer whom Churchill particularly loved.'

General Sir Bernard Paget

'I don't ask opinions, I give orders.'

Arthur Harris

BOMBER HARRIS

In February 1942, partly as a result of the Butt Report, the Air Ministry published the Area Bombing Directive. It was now permissible to hit cities 'without restriction.' On 22 February 1942 Air Marshall Arthur Harris was appointed Commander-in-Chief of RAF Bomber Command. He was regarded as a hard man for hard times. Someone who finally could - and would - get the job done where others had failed.

Arthur Harris was born in England in 1892, but emigrated to Rhodesia in 1910 to become a farmer. In 1915, he returned to England and signed up for service in the Royal Flying Corps. By 1917, he was Squadron Leader of No.45 Squadron flying Sopwith Camel fighters. He stayed with the RFC when it became the Royal Air Force and by the time the

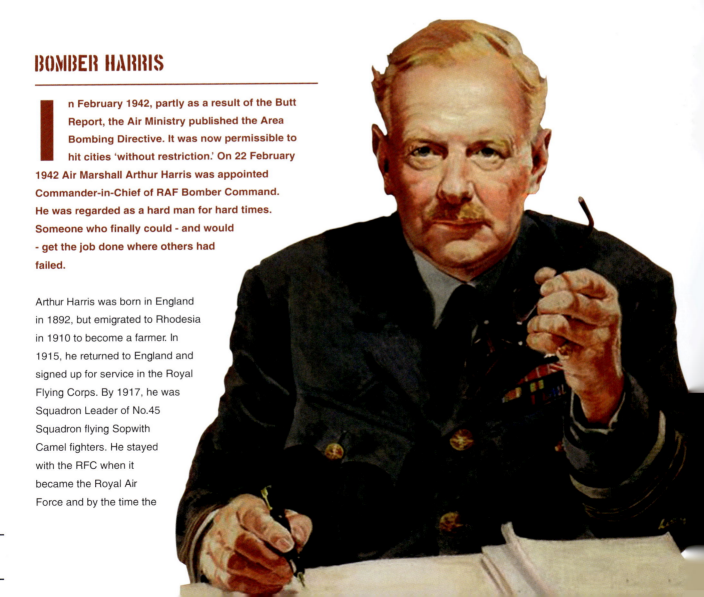

war was over Harris was a major with five confirmed kills to his credit. He served throughout the Empire in the 1920s and 1930s. While on Empire duty, he became interested in bombing techniques, helping to develop delay-action bombs, the use of *'Area Bombing'* in Iraq and creating his own designs for bomb racks. He started to develop a true faith in the bomber as a war-winner, commenting during the Arab Revolt in Palestine that *'one 250 lb. or 500 lb. bomb in each village that speaks out of turn'* would soon settle matters.

ABOVE: Aerial photo showing the bombing of a German U-boat or submarine base in Pola, Italy, during World War II

LEFT: RAF Air Chief Marshal Sir Arthur Harris

In 1938 he commanded No. 4 (Bomber) Group and campaigned for large bombers as opposed to light and medium types. When the Second World War broke out, he was next put in charge of No.5 Group and then appointed head of RAF Bomber Command in February 1942. He was ordered to carry out the new tactic of *'Area Bombing'* (also called *'Saturation Bombing'*) ordered by Churchill and the War Cabinet and became its most ardent advocate. Churchill had called for *'an absolutely devastating, exterminating attack by very heavy bombers from this country upon the Nazi homeland'.* By now, Air Staff policy had hardened considerably. German towns and cities were to be made *'physically uninhabitable'* and the German populace to be *'conscious of constant personal danger'.* Area Bombing was the tactic whereby Bomber Command would attempt to destroy Germany's industrial capability and shatter the morale of its largely civilian workforce. This goal, said the government should be given *'…priority over all other commitments'.* Harris set to work carrying out his orders.

'If you can't hit the works, hit the workers.'

Arthur Harris

Harris was a difficult man. He was blunt, stern, argumentative and sublimely self-assured. Tact, diplomacy, charm and guile were not tools he would - or could - employ. He hated a lot of people including Arabs, Americans, the British Army, the British Navy and even RAF Fighter Command for its seeming inability to distinguish *'between friendly and hostile aircraft'*. He hated civil servants and men from the ministry. *'Morning Abrahams,'* he is alleged to have called out to someone in the corridors of power, *'and what have you done to impede the war effort today?'* He hated Germans too. To him *'a Hun was a Hun'* and he made little distinction whether that Hun was in uniform or not. He had few personal friends, but it was to his credit that he well liked by the men who flew under his command as well as by American air commanders who were now starting to join the fray. He was just shy of fifty, on his second marriage and suffered constantly from ulcers. His few loves included mules, cooking and chain smoking Camel cigarettes.

The Bomber Command that Harris inherited had less than four hundred aircraft - very few of which were the heavier four-engine bombers he so wanted. He set to work on enlarging Bomber Command's fleet - and its striking power. Barely three months after taking over Bomber Command, Harris was able to hurl his first *'1,000 bomber raid'* against Cologne. It was a triumph for him, but he understood he had nowhere near-enough aircraft to destroy Germany. 1942 would be, as Harris put it, *'a year of preparation.'* He would bomb as wide a range of targets as possible, making the Nazis unable to export their fighter planes, soldiers and artillery to the Eastern Front. They would be needed for home defence.

'We are going to scourge the Third Reich from end to end. We are bombing Germany city by city and ever more terribly in order to make it impossible for them to go on with the war. That is our object; we shall pursue it relentlessly.' - Arthur Harris, Radio Address July 1942.

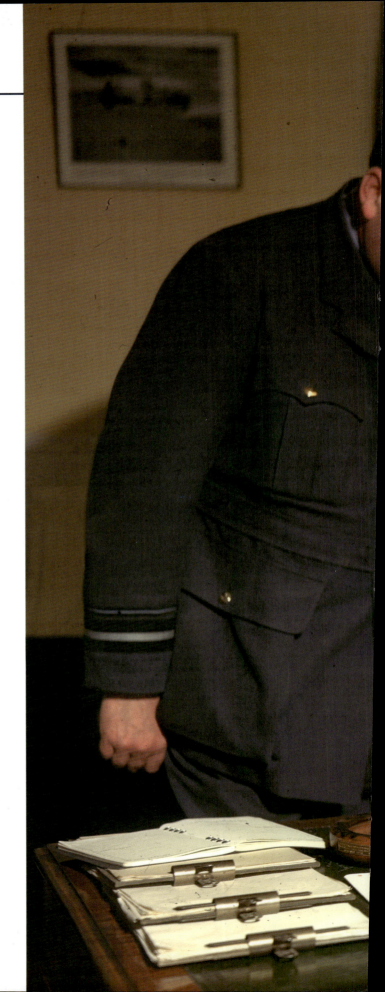

BELOW: Arthur Harris (seated), Commander in Chief Bomber Command; Air Vice Marshal R.H.M.S. Saunby (left), Senior Air Staff Officer; Air Commodore R. Harrison (right) Deputy Senior Air Staff Officer

INTO SERVICE

The first three Lancaster B.1's - L7537, L7538 and L7541- arrived at RAF Waddington, Lincolnshire, on Christmas Eve, 1941, assigned to No 44 (Rhodesia) Squadron. Waddington already had a single prototype Lancaster - BT308 - in residence since September 1941 for the purposes of air and ground crew training. It took no time at all for the men of 44 Squadron to realise that their new Lancasters were far superior to the Handley Paige Hampdens they had been flying. Shortly after, more Lancasters arrived to reequip 44 and then 97 Squadron which shared Waddington with 44 Squadron.

Of those iconic first three Lancasters delivered to 44 Squadron on Christmas Eve, only one - L7541 - survived until the end of the war. L7538 crash-landed in February 1942 but its crew all escaped. The crew of the third Lancaster, L7537, were all killed when their Lancaster was shot down while bombing Dusseldorf on 31 July 1942. No.44 Squadron would fly over 4,350 Lancaster sorties over the duration of the war. 149 of its Lancaster were shot down and a further 22 were lost in accidents or crash-landings. The Squadron had the dubious distinction of suffering the highest Lancaster losses in RAF Bomber Command. By October 1942, Bomber Command would have nine Lancaster squadrons. 516 aircraft would be built in 1942.

On the night of 3/4 March 1942, four Lancasters of 44 Squadron flew the bomber's very first combat operation, taking off from the grass runways at Waddington at 6.15pm. Their mission was to sew mines in the Heligoland Blight area against German shipping. All returned safely.

INSET: Prototype Lancaster - BT308

MAIN IMAGE: Three Avro Lancaster B Mark Is of 44 Squadron, Royal Air Force based at Waddington, Lincolnshire, flying above the clouds. Left to right: W4125,`KM-W', being flown by Sergeant Colin Watt, Royal Australian Air Force; W4162,`KM-Y', flown by Pilot Officer T G Hackney (later killed while serving with No 83 Squadron); and W4187,`KM-S', flown by Pilot Officer J D V S Stephens DFM, who was killed with his crew two nights later during a raid on Wismar

ESSEN

Just over a week later, two Lancasters of 44 Squadron flew their first bombing mission. The target was the Krupp munitions centre in Essen, Germany, and they were to join a mixed force of RAF bombers 126 strong including Wellingtons, Hampdens, Stirlings and Manchesters. Each Lancaster went out with 5,000lbs of incendiaries in their bomb bays. Both Lancasters returned safely. Two more attacks on the city followed.

The second of these three attacks on Essen was considered at the time to have been very successful. Fires were started in Krupps' Works and oil storage cisterns believed to have been destroyed. Individual crews reported fires in the target area which looked like whole streets ablaze and a fire of great size near a railway junction. On the preceding and subsequent nights however bad weather precluded accurate identification of the primary targets and the bomber force accidentally struck at least 24 different German towns.

GEE

The chaos over Essen came despite the first use of GEE, fitted to a single Wellington.

Gee was an attempt to overcome the problems the RAF had with navigating, especially at night. It was originally devised by Robert Dippy in 1940 to help bombers find the runway on the way home, but experiments showed that it had far greater range than expected. It was then further developed as a long range navigation system to help bombers find their target cities, by measuring the time delay between two radio signals to produce a 'fix'.

ABOVE LEFT: Production of Tiger I tanks at the Krupp factory, Essen during World War II

ABOVE CENTRE AND RIGHT: GEE Transmitter (left) and GEE airborne equipment (right) At RAF Air Defence Museum

MAIN IMAGE: Avro Lancaster Mark I, L7578, KM-B, of No.44 (Rhodesia) Squadron, Royal Air Force, in flight over the Lincolnshire countryside on 14 April 1942, while practising for the low-level attack on the M.A.N. diesel engineering works at Augsburg which took place on 17 April

AUSBURG

On 17 April, six Lancasters of No.44 Squadron and a further half-dozen from 97 Squadron launched a daring precision daytime raid against the MAN U-boat Diesel engine factory in Augsburg in Germany, sweeping in at tree top height to attack. Each aircraft carried four 1,000lb bombs. '

The raid was a pyric victory at best. Seven of the twelve Lancasters were lost mostly to Bf.109 and Fw.190 interceptors - an absolutely unsustainable rate of attrition. It proved beyond all reasonable doubt to Harris that, even with a superior aircraft like the Lancaster, unescorted precision daylight raids were still not feasible.

Despite this, the British government chose this raid to announce the existence of the Lancaster to the general public. Afterwards, the leader of the raid told the BBC;

'We Lancaster crews believe that in the Lancaster we have got the answer for heavy bombing.'

> *'Over the target there were so many aircraft that we could have done with traffic lights.'*
>
> Rear Gunner 'Chan' Chandler

OPERATION MILLENNIUM · THE THOUSAND BOMBER RAID

Harris wanted to do it big, and so he begged, stole and borrowed men and machines from just about everywhere to launch his first '1000' Bomber Raid'. In secret, he hoped that the spectacle would make the Germans sue for peace.

The target chosen for the night of 30/31 May 1942 was the German City of Cologne and 73 Lancasters took part out of close to 1,000 planes. They flew in high and in the light of a brilliant full moon. Six hundred acres of the city were flattened and burned, as the massive bomber waves dropped over 2,000 tons of bombs of which 2/3rds were incendiaries. The city burned from end to end and the Lancasters coming in for the third wave glowed vivid red reflecting the fire below. Returning bombers could look back and see Cologne burning from 100 miles away. 486 Germans died and another 200,000 were evacuated. It was estimated that industrial production in the area had been set back a month and the raid was a huge propaganda victory for the RAF. The British public loved it, the Americans admired it and even the grudging Soviets were a little thankful for the support. Goering declared it an impossibility. Churchill and Portal were awestruck. Of the thousand bombers, only 43 were lost. Arthur Harris was given a knighthood on 11 June 1942.

Lancasters continued flying on Bomber Command missions throughout the summer and autumn. They were used more and more for conventional night raids, but were also lent out for the occasional coastal patrol, mine-laying duties or to attack German shipping - a task Harris dismissed as just *'frightening cod.'* On 17 July, a 61 Squadron Lancaster actually managed to sink a German U-boat. Mine-laying missions were often coded as 'Gardening', and tended to get assigned to novice crews for experience. Hamburg, Stuttgart, Mannheim, Duisburg, and Munich were all targets struck by Lancaster forces during the latter part of the year, as well as targets in Italy

including Turin, Milan, and Genoa. In 1942, 75% of all ops were flown against German targets.

Due to a shortage of Merlin Engines, the first Lancaster B.II - using Bristol Hercules engines - made its first flight in November. It was not as good as the Merlin-equipped variant. It had a lower operational ceiling, a smaller bombload and a slower speed. After 301 were built by Armstrong-Whitworth it was decided that no more would follow.

ABOVE: Official British war art imagining a bombing raid on Cologne. The city's cathedral is clearly visible. It survived the war, despite being hit dozens of times by Allied bombs

BELOW: A ground crew refuelling and reloading a Lancaster bomber, 4th September 1942

1942

THE PATHFINDERS

During the Blitz of 1940/41, the Luftwaffe had developed a tactic to get their bombers close to target by night. An elite squadron was assembled to fly ahead of the main force and illuminate the target with flares. The regular bombers following up would therefore be able to home in on the illuminated area.

In 1941 as the RAF still struggled with the same task of trying to find targets by night, Group Captain Syd Bufton from the Air Ministry suggested that Britain too form its own elite squadrons to bring the main bombing force to the target. He was secretly hoping that eventually Bomber Command could resume precision bombing and dispense with area bombing. Harris was not a fan of the idea (and didn't like Bufton much either). He believed that the idea of an 'elite' within Bomber Command would cause dissent in the ranks and damage morale. His preferred solution instead was to have one or two aircraft in each squadron take on the task. There was much support for Bufton's idea. One of the government's chief scientists, Sir Henry Tizard, famously said:

'I do not think the formation of a first XV at rugby union makes little boys play any less enthusiastically.'

Harris was well and truly overruled. He greatly outranked Bufton - but Bufton had friends in high places. Harris most certainly did not. In August 1942, aircrew began to be transferred out of their squadrons (after clandestine interviews, usually down the pub) and into the newly formed Pathfinder Force (PFF) under the command of Australian Group Captain Don Bennett. Five squadrons of Pathfinders were originally established - one for each of the five bomber groups. Lancasters were the chosen aircraft for No.5 Group and 83 Squadron, stationed at RAF Wyton, who had recently ditched their Manchesters after just four months. Other groups had Mosquitoes, Stirlings, Halifaxes and Wellingtons assigned to them. Crews were given a temporary raise in rank and pay.

The fledgling Pathfinder Force first saw action on the night of 18/19 August 1942. 31 PFF aircraft including Lancasters from 83 Squadron led the raid, with the main force of around 85 mixed bomber types following. Their destination was to be Flensburg, considered by the RAF to be a soft and easy target and perfect for a first try. There was initially great excitement when the bombers returned. 16 PFF aircraft claimed to have successfully illuminated the target and 78 of the other bomber crews claimed to have bombed it. It would have been a major success - had their claims been true. What really happened was that strong winds had blown the Pathfinders 25 miles north of their intended route - and the whole force ended up bombing Demark by mistake. Fortunately, they didn't hit much on the ground and only four Danes were hurt.

ABOVE LEFT: 83 Squadron aircrew in front of their Lancaster R5868, Squadron Leader Shailendra Eknath Sukthankar, an Indian Navigator stands in the middle, 28 February 1942

RIGHT: Australian Group Captain Don Bennett

The supporters of the PFF were not daunted. They were sent out again on the night of 24/25 August - this time to find Frankfurt. Again the mission was far from a success. Heavy clouds confused the Pathfinders and they ended up illuminating some fields and villages to the north and west of the city. Some bombs actually fell on Frankfurt, mostly by accident, and killed and injured several people and started a few fires. The cost of the raid was heavy. Five PFF aircraft were lost, alongside six Lancasters, five Wellingtons, four Stirlings and a Halifax. This comprised over 7% of the entire raiding party - and questions began to be asked about the efficacy of the PFF itself.

It was fortunate for the PFF and its supporters that the raid on Kassel, on the night of 27/28 August, went well. Cloud cover over the target was very light. The Pathfinder aircraft were able to locate it with some precision and illuminated it well. The following bomber force hit it hard and true. All three factories belonging to the Henschel aircraft company were severely damaged. 28 German soldiers were also killed when their barracks was hit. The one thing that spoiled the raid was the high attrition rate. 31 Allied aircraft out of a total strength of 306 were lost - over 10% of the RAF bomber force that had set out. 5% was considered the absolute limit.

There was no time to pause and take stock. The very next night the PFF were back out again, as 159 bombers set off for a low altitude raid on Nuremberg. The Pathfinders once more found their target and illuminated with great accuracy - but results were mixed. Only fifty of the raiders actually bombed on target and some ordnance fell as far away as 10 miles to the north. Once again, the bombers took a mauling. 23 were shot down. They comprised a shocking 14.5% of the total strength sent on the raid. Many of the aircraft lost were old Wellingtons - and the nearly obsolescent bombers accounted for 34% of all Allied losses.

The night of 1 September saw the PFF leading a mission of some 231 bombers against Saarbruken. Unhappily, the PFF illuminated the nearby town of Saarlouis instead. The next night though, 200 bombers were led successfully to the town of Karlsruhe. Over 200 fires in the target area were reported and a high number of homes were destroyed.

Now, the PFF started to re-evaluate their tactics. Pathfinder aircraft would be split into three. Those designated as 'Illuminators' would drop white illuminations along the approach to the target to guide the main force in. Next, 'Visual Markers' would drop coloured flares over the target itself before 'Fire Starters' came in loaded with incendiaries to further mark the target. It worked. On the night of 4/5 September, 251 aircraft set off to bomb Bremen with the PFF in the lead. Cloud cover was light and the Pathfinders dropped their flares and incendiaries accurately. 460 worker homes were bombed out completely and almost 9,000 others damaged. There were also notable hits on the Weser aircraft works and the Atlas shipyard complex of warehouses.

The Germans needed a solution to the RAF's newfound accuracy and came up with a plan to confuse the bombers by planting dummy indicators safely away from the target. This new tactic almost completely wrecked an assault on Cologne by 289 aircraft on the night of 15/16 October. Enticed away from the city, the bombers expended 70,000 bombs on the countryside. Just over 200 bombs (including a high percentage of small incendiaries) found the target. Bomber Command were going to need an answer - and quickly.

ABOVE: German soldier and a civilian observing fires ravaging Fieseler aircraft plant at Bettenhausen, a suburb of Kassel, Germany, after bombing by R.A.F. and the U.S. Eighth Air Force

ABOVE INSERT: The Pathfinder wings worn beneath the aircrew flying badge by members of Pathfinder Force

BELOW: Sectional fuselage model of a 1942 Avro Lancaster

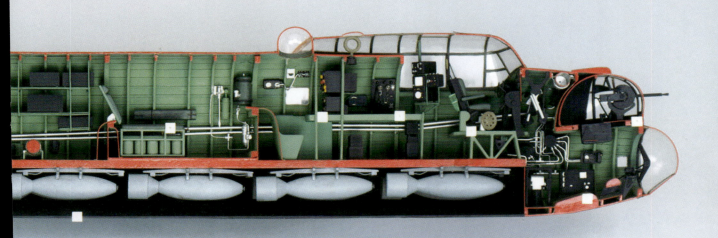

OBOE

Oboe was yet another attempt to make bombing raids more accurate in what was becoming ever more a technological battle. Developed by A H Reeves & F E Jones it was called Oboe because of the distinctive noise it made. An aircraft fitted with Oboe flew along a beam provided by a ground station back in England. At the same time, another beam transmitted by a second, 'Mouse' station would focus on the target. When the two beams crossed, the bombers dropped their payloads.

Oboe came with drawbacks. Firstly, it had a maximum range of 300 miles. This was adequate for bombers hitting the Ruhr, but it meant that it could not provide help on missions of greater range, such as attacks on Berlin to the east. There were only two stations in the whole of Britain to begin with and the entire two station system could only handle a dozen bombers every hour. To get the best accuracy from Oboe, planes had to fly straight and level for several minutes right over the target, making them particularly vulnerable to searchlights and flak. Because of the strict limits on its aircraft handling capabilities, it was assigned just to a Pathfinder aircraft, usually a Mosquito. Early results were mixed but encouraging enough to continue with and within months it was claimed that the system helped bombers to drop their bombs within 600 yards of their target, given ideal operating conditions.

MAIN IMAGE: Avro Lancaster heavy bomber R5689 (VN-N), of No. 50 Squadron RAF, in flight during World War II, 1942. The aircraft was delivered to 50 Squadron in June 1942, but was destroyed when it crashed on landing at Thurlby, Lincolnshire on 19th September that year

RIGHT TOP: The Telecommunications Research Establishment (TRE) at Malvern in Worcestershire where the system was developed in 1942

RIGHT MIDDLE: An illustration of Oboe being used

RIGHT BOTTOM: The left side of this image shows an Oboe navigation console. The two CRTs, some of the largest built during that era, were used for gross and fine distance measurement

1942

63

BACON EGGS AND CHOP GIRLS LANCASTER AIR CREW

'Courage, confidence and character' were the three traits Bomber Command looked for in aircrew.

125,000 pilots and crew served with Bomber Command during the Second World War. Over 55,000 of them would die.

Each man was a volunteer. By 1942, they were mostly civilians, the professionals having been killed already. 5,000 of them died just in training. They came from 60 different countries. One in every four air crew came from the Dominions. The West Indies contributed over 500 airmen and it never failed to shock the Germans when a captured British airman turned out to be black. There were Czechs, Poles and Frenchmen, all eager to strike back, a handful of Peruvians too, and even Germans who hated fascism. It was originally intended that 'foreign' crew members should fly in dedicated national squadrons (also known as Article XV Squadrons), but many found themselves attached to regular units and diverse crews did indeed achieve the best results. More than a million men and women supported them on the ground.

The age of pilots and crew usually ranged from 19 to the mid-twenties. On average, they were 21 years old. The average age at which they died was 23. The youngest known air crew was 16-year-old Flight Sergeant Edward Wright who died aboard a Lancaster of No.428 'Ghost' Squadron RCAF, barely days before the war ended. In early 1943, just 17% of men could hope to survive their first tour of thirty sorties. They would then enjoy six months grace before returning to active duty. The chance of surviving a second tour was 2.5%. Crews assigned to Pathfinder Squadrons were expected to fly a tour of 45 operations.

25% of the men were of officer rank. Predictably, almost every volunteer wanted to be a pilot. As might be expected, there was some class prejudice with pilots, bomb aimers and navigators being recruited from university or grammar school backgrounds. This was especially true of the Air Ministry who thought that the well-bred and privately educated made the best aircrew. As the war progressed however, they had no choice but to accept the 11+ scholarship boys - intelligent, raw, complex and intense young men who would preoccupy playwrights a decade later. Rough and cocky Colonial aircrew were considered almost beneath contempt by the Ministry. Nevertheless it was common for a pilot to be an NCO and another crewman to be an officer. Tradition had it that the lower ranking man saluted his superior once a day and then they forgot all about it. Crews were usually fiercely bonded and would socialise together, regardless of background or rank. Some even went on leave together. Most had chosen each other as crewmates while at their Operational Training Units. The men were cynical and hardened - but still church services on a Sunday were always well attended. Many had premonitions of their own deaths.

Down at RAF High Wycombe, Harris would usually announce the day's targets at around 9am in his underground Ops Room nicknamed *'The Hole'*. Selecting

a target involved studying photo reconnaissance and intelligence data, gathering meteorological predictions, specifying bomb types and loads and assessing fuel requirements. The process was known as '*Morning Prayers*' and always initiated by Harris lighting a cigarette. Immediately after, Harris would stalk back to his office where he felt happiest while Saunby, his devoted deputy and model railway aficionado, attended to the finer details. Harris usually put in 16 hour days.

A typical Lancaster air field in 1942 had around 2,500 personnel and almost everyone went everywhere by bike. They were typified by low Nissan huts and acres of foul mud. There was good food for the aircrew, but ground staff might receive a plate of fish paste.

Usually no-one had any idea whether or not they would be flying that night until 'Battle Orders' were posted on

ABOVE: Aircrew and groundcrew of Avro Lancaster KB760 NA:P "P-Peter", from No. 428 Squadron RCAF. The badge for the Imperial Order of the Daughters of the Empire is visible on the nose. Photo taken after the squadron's 2,000th sortie, a raid on Bremen, Germany

LEFT: No. 428 Squadron RCAF badge

a noticeboard mid-morning. This would not only set out the aircraft due to fly but also the individual members of each crew. If their names were not listed, airmen could essentially '*go and play*' for the day. Once they knew they were on for ops, a crew would quickly 'air test' their bomber to ensure it was working safely. On the ground, the bomber's personal 'Erks' (Ground crew) would be on standby to correct any deficiencies the pilot and crew discovered during the 'air test'. Erks considered that the bomber actually belonged to them and - when a crew took it out on a mission - they were only borrowing it. If their aircraft was U/S or unserviceable, crew might well be assigned a spare bomber for the night's mission. This was considered jolly back luck - and tempting the fates.

Now bombers out on the perimeter would be fuelled up, with bowsers filling their wing tanks and the bomb bay 'bombed up' with tonight's ordnance. Guns were freshly loaded with ammo. All tasks were double-checked by the ground crew NCO.

The airfield was locked down tight and closed to most traffic in or out to help maintain secrecy. Public telephones on the airfield were padlocked. With RAF police guarding the doors, pilots and navigators then filed into the briefing room. Facing them, usually on a stage, was their CO, accompanied by the flight commanders, an intelligence man and a Meteorology officer. A map of Europe was then unveiled, revealing the target as well as the flight path to and from their destination. The map also showed the locations of known searchlight batteries (in green) and flak batteries (In red). After the navigation briefing, the rest of the crew were invited to join their crewmates and hear the rest of the briefing.

There was some free time now to compose letters home to family or sweethearts, try to get some rest and have a meal. The more sardonic of crew members referred to this as '*the Last Supper*'. It was common knowledge that losses were continuing to be very, very high. Portal was trying to keep it a state secret, but it was impossible. Fatalism and gallows humour prevailed.

Time to get ready. Parachutes and life preservers were collected from the Parachute Section' ('*If it doesn't work, bring it back*' was a popular joke) before the men dressed in the 'Crew Room', where boiled sweets, chocolate, coffee thermoses and sandwiches were handed out . Pockets were emptied of all personal effects just in case they were shot down and captured - and many a lucky charm would be checked and double checked for its

comforting presence by at least 80% of airmen. Rabbit's feet, teddy bears and lucky scarves were all popular. It wouldn't do to fly without them. As casualties mounted, certain bunks or sleeping quarters became considered unlucky, as perhaps would be the designation 0-0range or R-Robert. At least one cockpit was decorated with two pairs of stolen women's panties. Even some WAAFs were judged to be jinxed. If you dated her, you died. They were known as '*chop girls*.'

WAAFs in trucks would then pick up aircrews and take them out to their bomber which sat dispersed on the airfield perimeter. Once the WAAFs had dropped them off, it was common for the crew to gather around their bomber's wheels and urinate on them. This was partly for good luck, partly because some men rather badly need to go given the ordeal facing them and party because it was exceptionally cold on the mission and difficult to rearrange yourself for the toilet. Given the state of stress many crews experienced, this toilet might well be very heavily used, particularly on the way home when sheer relief and desperate exhaustion set in. 'Erks in particular hated them. It was their job to clean them out.

After the urination ceremony, it was time to climb aboard. More checks would be made on the aircraft. The engines were 'run up' and a sheet containing Form 700 was filled out and handed to the ground crew chief as proof that the crew were happy with the condition of the aircraft.

German intelligence could possibly listen in to R/T chatter, even from the continent, so talk was kept to a minimum - mostly to check that the comms were working and that the crew members were ok. Instead a traffic light system provided visual indication. Once summoned, the pilot taxied his aircraft out and awaited the signal to take off. The gap between bombers taking off was usually one minute. If anything went wrong at this stage there was little to no chance of survival for anyone on board. A 30 ton bomber loaded to the gills with fuel, bombs and ammunition crashing at 130 miles an hour wasn't something anyone wanted to contemplate.

The pilot would take his aircraft up to its designated height

ABOVE: The crew of an Avro Lancaster of No. 57 Squadron RAF eat their bacon and eggs at Scampton, Lincolnshire, after returning from a raid

LEFT: A wireless operator of an Avro Lancaster bomber operating from Waddington, Lincolnshire carrying two pigeon boxes. Homing pigeons served as a means of communications in the event of a crash, ditching or radio failure

and then off to the Group's assembly point, probably somewhere near the English coast. Bombers based north of the Humber usually left England via Flamborough Head, while those based to the South went overhead and out over the North Sea at Cromer. While flying over the sea, the gunners briefly tested their guns, while other crew members shouted to the navigator if they spotted any landmarks.

The pilot calling '*Enemy coast ahead*' was usually the

first indication that the fun and games were about to begin. There were flak ships waiting for them off the coast of Europe and if they were spotted a brief but furious flak barrage would commence. Past the flak ships, the crews now started to worry about German night fighters, either being directed to them to by ground-based radar or increasingly using their on-board radar to hunt down a bomber. There were an estimated 162 night fighters - mostly Ju.88s and Bf.110s defending Germany at the start of 1942. By the end of the year, numbers had more than doubled. Pilots would bank every few minutes to help their gunners see more of the sky. Everyone who could kept an eye out in the darkness for any sign of fighters, while the navigator duly noted the position of any friendly bomber reported to be shot down. There were other dangers too out there in the dark - mostly the threat of colliding with another bomber. There might be hundreds of them, all completely invisible in the darkness. A bomber suddenly being attacked by an enemy fighter might take wild evasive action - and slam right into the bomber next to him, destroying them both in a heartbeat. Banks of well-disciplined searchlights were also a hazard. Once 'coned' in a searchlight, a bomber would be a relatively easy target for night fighters or flak gunners. To escape, the pilot would usually try a rapid descending corkscrew manoeuvre. Searchlight operators found it difficult to keep the plane in their beams, and enemy fighters couldn't match the manoeuvre because the stresses on their air frames would rip them to pieces. Inside a Lancaster taking violent evasive action it was not uncommon for half the crew to throw up. The plane would reek of vomit for the rest of the mission.

Now the crews were pressed to exhibit what Harris called, *'the two o'clock in the morning courage of lonely men...'* Things only intensified where the bombers reached their TAs or Target Areas. They were usually greeted by the thickest concentration of searchlights and gun batteries

ABOVE: A WAAF signals officer tests the intercom system in an Avro Lancaster

RIGHT: 'The Style for You is Air Force Blue!' was a recruitment booklet produced for the WAAF. Describing potential recruits as 'partners in victory'

encountered so far. In later missions, bombers would be expected to 'Stooge around' (fly in circles) until their turn to come in was called by a 'Master Bomber' from his aircraft. Now the bomb run began, heading for the Pathfinder flares illuminating the TA with the bomb aimer lying on his belly in his forward position (with a steel helmet below him to protect his genitals) giving frantic last minute course corrections to the pilot as they closed with the target. Below them the entire city would seem to be a fiery red carpet, punctuated with large explosions. The plane had to be straight and level now, just the way the enemy gunners and night fighters liked it. As the Bomb Aimer yelled *'Bombs gone!'*, the aircraft would suddenly leap several hundred feet straight up in the air from the drastic loss of weight. At the same time, a violent camera flash went off to record where the bombs were falling. Once over the shock, the pilot would typically turn and dive, heading for home just as fast as possible. In 1942, individual aircraft abandoned their streams and found their individual ways home, flying faster now because of reduced weight. The navigator would plot a course the best he could to avoid known trouble spots plagued by guns, searchlights or prowling enemy fighters out looking for easy kills - stricken bombers limping home with damaged engines. The Luftwaffe often chased them right across the North Sea, and exhausted air crew usually took their prescribed amphetamines at this stage of the mission to keep them sharp and alert. If there was any coffee and sandwiches left, they would almost invariably be frozen solid. Some wireless operators tuned in to radio stations and played dance music for the crew. Once below the height where oxygen was needed, many a cigarette was lit, quite against regulations.

Now the surviving bombers neared their home airfields. Landing priority was given to those aircraft with the least fuel, battle damage or with one or more wounded crew men aboard. Those who could not reach home made for other airfields closer to them. Aircraft were also commonly diverted elsewhere if home landing conditions were foggy or otherwise dangerous.

Once landed, crews were picked up and ferried to debriefing in the Ops Room. Ambulances took away the wounded. Mugs of tea or hot chocolate were thrust into cupped hands as the crews were interviewed about the facts of the night's raid. More than a few cigarettes were smoked and the rum passed around generously. Debriefing generally took 20 minutes. Then it was off to a post op meal - bacon, chips and eggs usually. There was usually extra milk too, sugar and fruit juices. The empty tables and chairs usually told the men who had *'got the chop'*. (Other sayings included *'gone for a Burton,'* which cheerfully suggested that the missing man was not dead but had simply popped out *'for a pint of Burton Ale'*). There was always some hope that they had diverted to another

BELOW: Lancaster B Mark III, LM449 PG-H, of No. 619 Squadron RAF based at Coningsby, Lincolnshire, in flight

station, or at that moment were furiously rowing a little rubber dinghy across the North Sea to Blighty, having ditched and thereby joined *'The Goldfish Club'* - but more often than not, empty chairs meant only one thing. The final confirmation would come with the removal of their personal effects from their rooms and the dreaded phrase *'missing as a result of air operations.'* Another 'sprog' crew would soon take their place. Their life expectancy now was just three weeks.

Many crew were so exhausted they fell straight to sleep but others drank heavily or took strong sedatives to help them sleep. Only another 29 missions to go, with the knowledge that the most hazardous flights were your first five (when you were still a sprog) - and your final five (when you were cocky).

Later in the war, one aghast senior officer observed of his men. *'Nobody was bothering about the length of their hair. They dressed like Desert Rats in their own idea of uniform.'* In the face of such constant danger, discipline was not appreciated. Rules were broken all the time. Some airmen took the occasional well-inebriated WAAF up with them on a mission. Others took their dogs. Colonials especially insisted on calling their senior officers by their first names.

It's estimated that around five and a half thousand air crew cracked under the strain and became *'flak happy'*. Some crews deliberately dropped their ordnance early to escape and became known as *'Fringe Merchants'*. Given sufficient R&R and good food, about a third made it back to active duty. The rest were branded as having LMF (Lack of moral fibre) and packed off to do menial tasks like toilet cleaning on another station where they could not affect morale.

'Everyone only had so much courage to give and you never knew when yours would run out.' - Arthur Cole, bomb aimer

If you said your prayers like a good boy and someone up there was listening, there might not be another mission that night. Maybe instead there'd be a raucous dance, mess party or variety show to enjoy. Lancaster aircrew were paid 10 shillings a day; an army private just 3 shillings. It could quite turn a girl's head. A night of fun. A film with gangsters in it, only pretending to be tough. A drinking contest. A chance to catch venereal disease. Again. Live fast. Die young.

1943

'At long last we were ready and equipped.'
Arthur Harris

READY TO GO

At the start of 1943, 100 Lancasters a month were being built. Production increased throughout the year and the first Canadian Lancaster Xs started arriving. It had 18 Lancaster squadrons by mid-summer 1943. Bomber Command was ready to get on with it.

On January 21, 1943, the Allies adopted the Combined Bomber Offensive directive. This directive provided for '*The progressive destruction and dislocation of the German military, industrial, and economic systems and the undermining of the morale of the German people to a point where their capacity for armed resistance is fatally weakened.*'

ON DISPLAY

In March 1943, the RAF put a Lancaster on display in Trafalgar Square as part of the Wings for Victory fundraising campaign. The public were awestruck. Over a million people came to see it on the first day, and donations by the end raised enough to pay for 315 Lancasters.

ABOVE: The crew of the first Canadian-built Avro Lancaster X to arrive in Britain, christened the 'Ruhr Express', photographed with their mascot at Northolt, Middlesex, on 15 September 1943

LEFT 'Wings For Victory Week' in London, March 1943

"LANCASTER" BOMBERS ARE SMASHING GERMAN INDUSTRIE

FOR FREEDOM

LEFT: WWII Lancaster Bomber poster

BRITAIN'S "LANCASTER" BOMBERS have made many flights over Germany, Italy and Occupied France. Bombing raids from British airfields are becoming heavier and heavier, not only by night but by day as well. By rendering many German-controlled war factories useless for production the war is being shortened. The "Lancaster" often carries Britain's giant 8,000 lb. bombs.

H2S

H2S was yet another attempt to provide an effective navigation aid and target-finding device to assist RAF Bomber crews. It was essentially a crude, downward facing radar device which could display a number of topographical features such as coastlines, rivers and the outlines of towns and cities. What it would mean, if it worked, was that bombers could travel deeper into the Reich and find their way more accurately, free of the limitations of Gee and Oboe.

ABOVE: Production H2S radar scope unit as flown during WWII

LEFT: Large areas like the Zuiderzee make excellent targets for the H2S. The resolution of the system is evident in the appearance of the Afsluitdijk (labelled "dam"), which is about 90 metres (300 ft) across'

Work on what was then called AIS began in early 1941. However, it was not until New Year's Day 1943 that the first 12 Stirling bombers and 12 Halifaxes had been equipped with the device. Active Operations began at the very end of that month with H2S-equipped Pathfinder bombers leading a 100 Lancaster raid on Hamburg. Unfortunately, less than a week later, an H2S - equipped Stirling was shot down during a raid on Cologne and the remains of H2S discovered by the Germans in the wreckage. They were mystified. Nothing like it had been found inside a Stirling before. They called it 'The Rotterdam Apparatus' and set to work backwards engineering it. It would take some time because of the damage and unfamiliar technology but ultimately German scientists would come up with the Naxos radar detector which enabled night fighters to actually home in on any aircraft using the system. Bomber Command responded with Boozer, which could detect night fighters emanating radar signals. Monica followed, an on board radar that detected German planes approaching from the rear. The German Flensburg system was then developed to track a bomber's Monica signals. And so it went.

INTO HAPPY VALLEY · THE BATTLE OF THE RUHR

The Ruhr region of Germany was one of the country's great industrial production centres. It also lay well to the west of the nation, within very convenient reach of Bomber Command airfields. It had been attacked for years, but a combination of strong ground defences, radar-directed night interceptors and a heavy pall of industrial smog hanging over the area made it a hard target. Bomber crews sourly named it *'Happy Valley'*. When Oboe became available, the smog cover became less of a problem. A test raid was conducted on Essen in January 1943 and proved successful. With Oboe-equipped Mosquito Pathfinders leading the way and marking targets, Harris was now confident he could launch a full blooded campaign against Germany's industrial heartland. 43 major bombing raids followed.

Throughout the campaign the Germans devoted more and more flak guns to the region's defences. By July 1943, almost 1/3 of all flak guns in Germany were located in the Ruhr, comprising over 1,000 large pieces and 1,500 smaller guns. 600,000 troops were required to man them. Despite this, it was the German night fighter cover that was to prove most deadly, accounting for around 70% of all bombers brought down. By July, 550 German combat aircraft were regularly defending the area.

The attack on the Ruhr officially began on the night of 5 March, when 442 bombers including 157 Lancasters streamed in to attack Essen with a mix of high explosives and incendiaries. Essen had been identified as the largest and most important manufacturing centre on the Ruhr region, with Krupps at its heart. Despite being guided by 8 Oboe-equipped Mosquitoes, only a third of the bombers managed to drop their ordnance within three miles of the target, and fourteen bombers were lost in the raid, four of them Lancasters. 53 separate buildings within the Krupps works were struck by bombs. Three nights later, the bomber force was over Nuremberg. The next day was Munich. The next major raid returned to Essen on the night of 12/13 March

ABOVE: Part of the locomotive shop of the Krupps AG works at Essen, Germany, seriously damaged by Bomber Command in 1943, and further wrecked in the daylight raid of 11 March 1945

as 156 Lancasters joined 158 Wellingtons, 91 Halifaxes, 42 Stirlings and ten Mosquitoes in a raid targeting the Krupps plant. 23 aircraft failed to return. A large-scale raid on Duisburg on 26/27 March largely failed in its objectives, due to problems with Oboe on board the Pathfinder Mosquitoes and heavy cloud cover over the target.

956 bombers were sent against Essen and other cities on the night of the 3/4 April. On 8/9 April, 392 bombers once again attacked Duisburg. 19 bombers were lost. The following night, 105 Lancasters led in by five Mosquito Pathfinders returned to the city but with only limited effect as the bombing was scattered. 8 Lancasters were lost on the raid. On 4/5 May, Bomber Command launched its first concerted strike on Dortmund with a force of 596 bombers.

1943

77

Bochum was the target on the night of 13/14 May with 442 bombers taking part. It's believed that German decoy flares led most of the bombers astray and the raid failed. 24 British bombers were lost.

On the night of 23/24 May, a raid by 826 bombers dropped 2,000 tons of high explosives and incendiaries on Dortmund in little under an hour. The important Hoesch steelworks ceased all production. British losses were put at 4.8%. The following night Dusseldorf was the main target for a force of 729 bombers. The bomber stream could not concentrate its ordnance due to heavy cloud cover and German decoy fires, and bombs rained down over a widely-scattered area. 26 bombers failed to return home. The night after that, Bomber Command returned its attention to Essen. 518 bombers took part in the raid, with 23 failing to return. Once again, bombing was scattered. Essen was hit, but so accidentally were ten other towns nearby. Just 24 hours later, 719 bombers struck at the relatively poorly-defended city of Wuppertal. Bombing was accurate and a 'firestorm' broke out at the centre of the 'Old Town'. 100,000 civilians found themselves homeless and five out of the six major factories in the city simply ceased to exist.

On the night of 11/12 June, 783 aircraft attacked Dusseldorf. The first wave hit their target, but when a Pathfinder Mosquito accidentally dropped its marker flares 14 miles to the north-east of the target, subsequent bomber waves were attracted to it and missed their true objective. 38 aircraft were lost and 140,000 Germans reportedly left homeless. The following night, the target was Bochum, and the city centre was virtually destroyed. 503 bombers took part. 24 aircraft failed to return. 24 hours later, a force of 197 Lancasters led by Oboe-equipped Mosquitoes struck at Oberhausen but casualties were relatively harsh. Some 4.8% of the raiding force did not

return home. Cologne was next, just 24 hours later. 212 bombers took part, led to the target this time by four-engine heavy Pathfinder aircraft using H2S. The H2S systems gave their operators trouble and there was heavy cloud cover over the city. Bombing was scattered over a wide area. 14 Allied aircraft were destroyed.

Krefeld was hit on the night of 21/22 June. 705 aircraft took part and Oboe-equipped Mosquitoes managed to mark the target area accurately, Bombers following them in started a massive fire that took several hours to bring under control. Unfortunately, the night was brilliantly illuminated by moonlight and the defenders managed to bring down 44 bombers. The next night, a force of 557 bombers destroyed an estimated 64% of Mulheim un dur Ruhr. Wuppertal was the target for a force of 630 bombers the following night. The Elberfeld region of the city was estimated to be 94% destroyed by the raid.

ABOVE LEFT: British propaganda leaflet dropped over Essen (Germany) after an RAF bombing raid in March 1943. The main title says "Fortress Europe has no roof". Imperial War Museum, London

ABOVE: The damaged fuselage and mid-upper turret of Avro Lancaster B Mark I, R5700 'ZN-G', of No. 106 Squadron RAF based at Elsham Wolds, Lincolnshire, after crash-landing at Hardwick, Norfolk, following an attack by a German fighter over Essen

Raids on the Nordstern oil plant at Gelsenkirchen, Gelsenkirchen itself and the city of Cologne were all plagued by problems with the Oboe systems on board the Pathfinders. In the latter Gelsenkirchen raid, Oboe failed on five out of six Pathfinder Mosquitoes and the one remaining Oboe system accidentally targeted an area some ten miles north of the target. There was greater success on the night of 25/26 July, when six hundred Bomber Command aircraft hit Essen once more, stopping all work at the entire Krupps factory.

The final raid of the campaign against the Ruhr came on the night of 30/31 July when Remscheid was attacked by 273 bombers. 15 were lost. In all, 26 German cities were attacked during the Battle of the Ruhr.

Bomber Command judged the Battle of the Ruhr to be a success, despite losing 872 aircraft. They dropped 58,000 tons of bombs. German aircraft production experienced a major set-back, there was a 'sub components crisis' and steel production was severely affected. It is estimated that around 15,000 Germans

1943

79

OPERATION CHASTISE – THE LANCASTER'S FINEST HOUR

'This squadron will either make history or be completely wiped out.'

Wing Commander Guy Gibson

While the Ruhr campaign was being waged in regular fashion, something of a spectacle took place; The Dambusters Raid.

Even before the war, the RAF had identified the hydro-electric dams of the Ruhr as potentially important targets in a future conflict with Germany. They provided everything from industry with power to clean drinking water. The problem was how to destroy them. It was accepted that RAF bombers could never hit them accurately, and they were well defended.

Barnes Wallis, the assistant chief designer at Vickers, had

been working on the concept of a special anti-shipping bomb for some time, and it was recognised that this might just be usable against dams. He preferred the idea of dropping a massive 10 ton bomb onto the dams from a high altitude but no RAF aircraft could lift the weight or reach the altitude required. Wallis rethought the problem. He understood that a much smaller bomb could do enormous damage, if it could only be exploded against the dam wall under the water - but the Germans had realised this and had protected the dams with anti-torpedo netting.

Once again, Wallis went away to think and returned with the concept of a very unusual bomb, code-named Upkeep. It would be a cylindrical 9000lb device with a hydrostatic fuse and designed to have a rapid backspin after release.

RIGHT: Portrait of Wing Commander Guy Gibson

BELOW: The most famous bombing raid by Lancasters was the 'Dambuster Raids'. For this, Barnes Wallis had to make a number of modifications to the Lancasters that took part in this raid. Nineteen Lancasters took part in this raid on May 17th 1943, with eight planes being lost

ABOVE: No. 617 Squadron practice dropping the 'Upkeep' weapon at Reculver bombing range, Kent before the attack on the Moehne, Eder and Sorpe Dams on the night of 16/17 May 1943

It would skip like a stone across the water, slam into the dam wall and sink underwater before exploding. However, it had to be released from any bomber at an optimum height of just 60 feet and a speed of 240 mph. After Wallis developed the initial idea by skipping his daughter's toy marbles across a water tub in his garden, official top secret trials began in May 1942. Scale model dams were blown up indoors in Watford, before an old, disused dam in Wales was struck and successfully breached by the bomb. Air Drop trials commenced at Chesil Beach in Dorset in December 1942, with a Wellington substituting for a Lancaster. Roy Chadwick joined Wallis to adapt the Lancaster to carry the revolutionary new bomb. To allow for the increased weight of the weapon, much of the Lancaster's protective armour was removed, as was the mid-upper turret. Gone too were the bomb bay doors. The bomb would have to be housed partially inside and partly outside of the aircraft. So adapted, the aircraft was designated as a Lancaster B Mark III Special (Type 464 Provisioning).

Wallis faced considerable opposition to his work. Harris wasn't particularly interested in the idea and said bluntly,

'This is tripe of the wildest description…there is not the smallest chance of it working.'

In the end, it was Air Chief Marshal Charles Portal who championed the project. He overruled Wallis's critics and gave the project his personal blessing in late February 1943. Harris was ordered to give up 30 of his Lancasters to the task. A provisional date for the raid was set for May, and No.5 Group were assigned the task.

Acting with speed, No.5 Group set up Squadron X. It was to be led by Wing Commander Guy Gibson. Despite being just 24-years-old, Gibson was already a veteran of an astounding 170 bombing and night-fighter sorties. He even went on missions he wasn't assigned to, just for the hell of it. Twenty one bomber crews were selected from No.5 Group Squadrons and the new squadron was assigned to RAF Scampton, close to the city of Lincoln where it officially became 617 Squadron.

Planners identified the Möhne and the Sorpe Dams as the main targets. The Eder Dam was selected as a secondary target. The task the crews faced was immense. They would have to navigate in the dark with almost unheard of precision, flying at ultra-low level over heavily-defended enemy territory. They would have to approach the dams at just the right angle, flying no more than 60 feet above the water and at the precise speed of 240 mph. The Upkeep bomb had to be released at just the right moment during the bombing run. One aircraft, just one bomb. RAF instruments were nowhere near accurate enough to allow such precise flying. Instead, two spotlights were mounted on the Lancasters, one on the nose and the other further back under the fuselage. When the two beams met, the aircraft was at 60ft.

Intense low level and night flying exercises began with Squadron X flying and practicing in secret. The Upkeep bombs arrived at Scampton on 13 May. Two days later, Gibson in the company of Barnes Wallis briefed his four most senior officers on the mission. The rest of the men received their briefings at 6pm on the 16th, shortly before the raid would commence.

The attacking force would be divided up into three formations of Lancasters:

The target for Formation One was the Mohne Dam. It comprised nine Lancasters, G-George flown by Gibson, M-Mother (Flt Lt Hopgood) and P-Popsie (Flt Lt H. B. 'Micky' Martin), A-Apple (Squadron Leader Melvin 'Dinghy' Young), J-Johnny (Flt Lt David Maltby), L-Leather (Flt Lt Dave Shannon), Z-Zebra (Sqn Ldr Maudslay), B-Baker (Flt Lt Bill Astell) and N-Nut (Pilot Officer Les Knight) . If any bombs were left over, the Lancasters carrying them would fly to - and attack - the Eder Dam.

Five Lancasters comprised Formation Two, which was assigned the Sorpe dam. The five pilots were Flt Lt Joe McCarthy in T-Tommy, P/O Vernon Byers in K-King , Flt Lt Norman Barlow in E-Easy, P/O Geoff Rice in H-Harry and Flt Lt Les Munro in W-Willie.

BELOW: "Upkeep" bouncing bomb mounted under Gibson's Lancaster B III (Special)

Formation Three was to act as a mobile reserve which would take off two hours after the other formations and then target any dams which had survived the main assault, or else three alternative, smaller ones - the Lister, the Ennepe and the Diemel. These five Lancasters would be piloted by Y-York (Flt Sgt Cyril Anderson), O-Orange (Flt Sgt Bill Townsend), F-Freddie (Flt Sgt Ken Brown RCAF), C-Charlie (P/O Warner Ottley) and S-Sugar (P/O Lewis Burpee RCAF). Illness ruled out two further crews from taking part.

The Operations Room was established at 5 Group Headquarters in St Vincents Hall, Grantham. They waited. The first Dambusters Lancasters took off from RAF Scampton at 9.28pm on May 16. Formation Two went first, as they were to fly the longer northern route to their target. McCarthy's bomber Q-Queenie (Better known as *Queenie Chuch-Chuck*) developed a coolant leak in one engine and he took off in the reserve aircraft T - Tommy 34 minutes late. Next to go was Formation One, with three aircraft clusters taking off at ten minute intervals from 9.39pm onwards. The reserve - Formation Three - did not set out until gone quarter past midnight on the 17th.

Formation One flew over the North Sea and then the Dutch coast, flying a complex and jagged route to avoid German fighter airfields, known flak gun concentrations and defences around the city of Hamm before turning south once more on-course for the Mohne. Despite this, they still encountered heavy flak and numerous searchlight batteries, causing Gibson to break radio silence to warn the aircraft behind him. They were racing now, flying at just 100 feet above the pitch black countryside below to dodge radar.

Formation Two crossed the continental coastline further north before adopting Formation One's route on target for the Sorpe dam. Les Munro's bomber was hit by flak. While the aircraft sustained little damage, radio comms on the bomber were knocked out and they were forced to head home. Rice's Lancaster, H-Harry, flew too low over the North Sea, actually swamping his bomb bay and knocking his bomb loose. Rice struggled to regain control as the bomb fell away completely into the water and managed to pull up. All the sea water he had taken aboard sloshed to the back and very nearly drowned the rear gunner in his turret. With no ordnance to drop, he headed for home too. Shortly after, Byer's Lancaster K-King was hit by flak and plunged into the Waddenzee with no survivors, while Barlow in E-Easy failed to spot electricity pylons just ahead of him and slammed into high voltage cables. Everyone died. Only T-Tommy which had taken off late, now survived from Formation Two.

LEFT: Eder Dam on 17 May 1943

RIGHT: Möhne Dam after the attack

Formation One also took a casualty, as pilot Astell in B-Baker also failed to spot power lines dead ahead of him inside Germany and ploughed into them. The aircraft reared up, burst into flames and dropped into the field below. Two minutes later, its Upkeep bomb exploded. Everyone on board was killed.

The surviving bombers of Formation One made it to the Mohne Dam. Guy Gibson in G-George started the first bombing run, screaming mad obscenities at the Germans as he brought his Lancaster down to just 60 feet above the inky-black waters of the Dam. The bomb was released and was dead on target - but for some reason it exploded harmlessly.

M-Mother went next. It was struck by flak from the gun towers on the dam, setting its outer port engine alight but still managed to get its bomb away. By great misfortune, it was just passing over the dam when its bomb went off directly below, smashing its port wing. It crashed shortly afterwards. Three members of the crew managed to parachute from the stricken bomber at just 500 feet, the rear gunner, bomb aimer and the wireless operator, but the wireless operator died shortly after and the other two were taken prisoner.

It was the turn of Martin now in P-Popsie. Gibson in G-George deliberately flew over the dam and its gun towers to draw away fire from P-Popsie as it came in. He was only partially successful. A gun tower managed to damage P-Popsie during its bomb run, but not enough to wreck things. Martin released his bomb and it was dead on target, sinking and then detonating on the under portion of the Dam.

A-Apple followed him in. Martin in P-Popsie came too, flying parallel with him, its guns blazing away at the flak batteries. All the guns had been loaded with tracer bullets, making the incoming fire look terrifying to the German gunners. 'Dinghy' Young again struck the damaged dam successfully.

Now P-Popsie and G-George escorted J-Johnny in on its bombing run, spraying fire at the gun towers. J-Johnny hit the target, spraying a spout of water a full thousand feet high over the dam. It still looked like the dam was holding, and Gibson was about to order Shannon in when the dam abruptly cracked and broke apart. Millions of gallons of water were released in a torrent. Back at HQ in Grantham, the comms were suddenly filled with wild screams and obscenities. For a moment, officers believed that some of the aircraft had been hit and they were listening to dying men's screams. Then the laughter started.

As the Mohne crumbled, Gibson led Shannon, Maudslay and Knight (who still had their bombs) on to the Eder some 12 minutes away. A-Apple followed them, Young thinking he might make a useful decoy when the bombing runs started. Maltby and Martin turned and set course for home.

The Eder dam proved a very different target. It was not defended by flak guns, but lay deep in mountainous terrain and was this night covered in fog. The approach proved both exceedingly difficult and perilous for the Lancaster crews. Shannon tried no less than six times to make a successful approach, but failed each and every time and got out of the way to let Z-Zebra try. Maudslay brought Z-Zebra in for a run, but he too was just off and his bomb exploded on top of the dam, lighting up the countryside for miles around and causing grave damage to his Lancaster as it flew overhead. Undaunted, Shannon came in again now and lined up perfectly. Despite this, his bomb fell short. Formation One had just a single Upkeep bomb left now, and it all was up to Knight in N-Nut. He came in, perfectly aligned, with Gibson flying beside him. The bomb dropped and hit its target. The dam slowly started to crack - and then it went.

The first two dams were made of concrete, but the Sorpe - the primary target of Formation Two was a huge, crude earthwork construction. Only one aircraft from the five Lancasters in Formation Two made it to the Sorpe - T-Tommy, piloted by Joe McCarthy. On approach at 12.15am, he found the terrain far more difficult and dangerous than he had anticipated. T-Tommy made no less than nine bombing runs against the dam. Each time, his bomb aimer called him off because the approach was not right. On the 10th run, the bomb aimer was satisfied and the bomb was dropped. It hit the dam, but only succeeded in damaging the top. It stood. Now, if the Sorpe was to be destroyed, it was all up to the Reserve in Formation Three.

Three of the reserve Lancasters had been ordered to target the Sorpe, but only two arrived. S-Sugar had already been crashed on its way to the target with the loss of all aboard, the pilot having been dazzled by a searchlight, and Y-York, trapped in dense fog and with damage to its rear turret, had already turned back. F-Freddie was alone.

The Lancaster went in but even after seven runs at the target still could not fly a successful approach. It was then he and his bomb aimer have an ingenious idea: They flew in again, this time dropping incendiaries, starting fires below. The fires in turn helped to lift the mist and on the 8th bomb run, F-Freddie was able to launch its bomb. It hit the target, sending great gouts of water 1,000 feet into the air but only succeeded in cracking the dam. It held.

The final two Lancasters of Formation Three had been vectored on to different targets. C-Charlie had been

BELOW: Flight Lieutenant Joe McCarthy (fourth from left) and his crew of No. 617 Squadron (The Dambusters) at RAF Scampton, 22 July 1943

RIGHT: Wing Commander Guy Gibson (Right) and S/Ldr David Maltby (left) at RAF Scampton, on 22 July 1943 after the raid

assigned the Lister dam, but was shot down by flak while on the way to the target. Struggling desperately with the controls, Pilot Officer Warner Ottley apologised to his crew: *'I'm sorry boys, they got us'*. Seconds later C-Charlie crashed, killing all aboard except the rear gunner, who survived because his tail section broke free.

The last bomber, O-Orange found and hit its target - the Ennepe Dam - but the bomb failed to cause any significant damage. On the way home, the crew could see some of the damaged inflicted by earlier strikes.

'All you could see were treetops and tops of houses. I thought it was just a miraculous sight to see all this water.' George Chalmers, wireless operator, 0-0range.

The surviving Lancasters turned and raced for home at little more than treetop height, but two more would be lost en route. Z-Zebra, already damaged, finally succumbed to flak over Holland and Dingy Young and his crew in A-Apple ran out of luck over Ijmuiden and were brought down by flak, crashing into the North Sea. All the crewmen died.

In all, eleven Lancasters came home after the raid. The first arrived just after 3am on the 17th and the last - O-Orange - at 6.15am, limping in on three engines. Air Chief Marshal Harris was there to welcome them back. 53 men had died - almost 40% of the crewmen who took part.

THE DAILY TELEGRAPH
'RAF BLOWS UP THREE KEY DAMS IN GERMANY'

THE DAILY MAIL
'FLOODS POURING THROUGH THE RUHR'

THE DAILY MIRROR
'HUNS GET A FLOOD BLITZ'

AFTERMATH

At first light, a photo-reconnaissance spitfire was despatched to discover the damage. The pilot later commented:

'*I looked down into the deep valley which had seemed so peaceful three days before but now it was a wide torrent. The whole valley of the river was inundated with only patches of high ground and the tops of trees and church steeples showing above the flood. I was overcome by the immensity of it.*' - Jerry Fray

At breakfast, it's said that waitresses at the canteen at Scampton openly wept at the sight of so many empty tables. Surviving aircrew were seen to be in a state of shock, milling around aimlessly or slumped over tables, their heads buried in their arms. They were all subsequently given a week's leave.

Barnes Wallis's wife recalled in a letter to a friend:

'Poor B. didn't get home till 5 to 12 last night, only 3 hours sleep Saturday, didn't take his clothes off Sunday, and was awake till 2.30 this morning telling me all about it. And then, poor dear darling Barnes, he woke at 6 feeling absolutely awful: he'd killed so many people.'

By Monday night, the raid was headline news on the BBC and the press followed suit the day after.

In June 1943, 34 Dambusters were decorated at Buckingham Palace. Leader of the raid Guy Gibson received the Victoria Cross. Others received five Distinguished Service Orders, 10 Distinguished Flying Crosses and four bars, two Conspicuous Gallantry Medals, eleven Distinguished Flying Medals and one bar.

Harris was still not impressed, saying:

'*I have seen nothing... to show that the effort was worthwhile except as a spectacular operation.*'

German civilians were shocked when they first heard of the raid and began referring to the '*Mohne catastrophe*'. The German authorities tried to blame the Jews for the raid and when people failed to believe them, described the raid as '*feeble*'. The true effect of the raid is difficult to judge. At least 1,650 died on the ground but many were foreign slave labourers. Industry was almost certainly disrupted - but what really mattered was the huge boost the raid gave to public morale in Britain.

After the raid, it was decided that 617 Squadron would

stay together as an elite specialist unit. They chose for themselves the Squadron motto: *Après moi le déluge* (*After me the flood*) with no little humour. Guy Gibson was killed flying Mosquitos in 1944.

WINDOW

German radar was an extremely important part of its defence co-ordination. It could help vector night interceptors onto incoming bomber streams, direct searchlight batteries or guide anti-aircraft batteries. Trying to confuse it was important.

The idea of Window was not new. It stretched back to 1937, when it was first realized that clouds of metal foil released from bombers might give confusing signals on enemy radar screens. Properly deployed it would give a signal identical to an actual bomber. With No.73 Squadron trained in its use, Harris chose to introduce Window on the first night of Operation Gomorrah. It proved an immediate success, effectively blinding German radar, causing mass confusion and undoubtedly cutting RAF losses by a very significant degree.

LEFT: No. 617 Squadron RAF badge

BELOW: King George VI visiting No. 617 Squadron in 1943

LEFT: An Avro Lancaster of No. 1 Group, Bomber Command, silhouetted against flares, smoke and explosions during the attack on Hamburg, Germany, by aircraft of Nos. 1, 5 and 8 Groups on the night of 30/31 January 1943. This raid was the first occasion on which H2S centimetric radar was used by the Pathfinder aircraft to navigate the force to the target. The pilot of the photographing aircraft (Lancaster 'ZN-Y' of No. 106 Squadron, based at Syerston) was Flt Lt D J Shannon who, as a member of No. 617 Squadron, took part in Operation CHASTISE (the "Dams Raid") during the following May

OPERATION GOMORRAH

'Then the Lord rained brimstone and fire on Sodom and Gomorrah, from the Lord out of the heavens.' - Genesis 19:24

Hamburg, Germany's northern second city, was always considered a very desirable target. It was relatively close to Britain, which not only meant that RAF bombers would spend less time exposed to night fighters and anti-aircraft batteries but also they would need fewer hours of darkness in which to hide. Hamburg could be bombed in summer. It was close to the coast and boasted a major river; both would act as navigation aids to a bomber force. It had U-Boat pens, important dock facilities and ship yards. It was rich in important industrial sites. But best of all, Britain's scientists decided that, because of the construction of many of the city's properties, it would burn like a roman candle. It was, they declared an *'outstandingly vulnerable target'*.

And so they decided to burn it.

On the night of 23/24 July 1943, 791 bombers including 354 Lancasters struck. RAF Pathfinders from No.35 squadron led the raid. Visibility was good and the new H2S worked well. The marker flares were dropped accurately and Window deployed for the very first time to knock out German radar. AA guns had to fire blind and fighters could not be vectored onto targets. Bombing commenced just before 01.00am and lasted for an hour, during which time 2,300 tons of incendiaries were dropped. Hamburg was protected by a very large and efficient fire fighting force of some 40,000 men. However the bombing destroyed the main telephone exchange and rubble swiftly jammed up the streets while burst mains wrecked water pressure. Even if the fire engines could be told where to go, getting there might still be impossible. As a result, some of the fires started on the night of 23/24 July were still burning out of control three days later. Over 1,500 people died. RAF losses amounted to just 12 aircraft (including four Lancasters), mainly thanks to the confusion caused by Window.

Hamburg was given no time to recover. At 16.40, ninety B-17s of USAAF's 8th Air Force rolled overhead in broad daylight, striking at the Blohm and Voss shipyard and an aircraft engine factory. The raid was not a success. Smoke obscuring the engine factory caused the bombers to miss altogether and the shipyards were not greatly affected. Anti-Aircraft fire on the other hand, succeeded in damaging 78 of the 90 Fortresses. Throughout the rest of the day, delayed action bombs from the previous night's RAF raid kept exploding in the city entirely at random, causing constant terror. Extra firemen from nearby Hanover were called in to help fight the many fires. The smoke from the first night's fires were now almost completely obscuring the city, and so the RAF called off their planned raid on Hamburg for the night of the 24/25 July. Instead, the 700 bombers prepared for the raid were sent off to bomb Essen.

The bombers returned to Hamburg just after midnight on 25/26 July but ran into freak weather. The skies over the North Sea were filled with lightning and severe winds made flying true almost impossible. Many bombers were forced to ditch their high explosive payload and then struggled on with just the 4lb incendiaries in their bomb bays. In the event, next to no meaningful strikes were reported in Hamburg.

The 26/27 July was a completely different story. The weather had greatly improved, and Bomber Command despatched 787 bombers against Hamburg. Wellingtons, Stirlings and Halifaxes all joined in, but by far the greatest numbers of aircraft taking part were now Lancasters - 353 of them. Tonight they meant business. The main targets were the crammed-in slums of the districts of Billwärder, Borgfelde, Hamm, Hammerbrook, Hohenfelde and Rothenburgsort - the places where the workers lived. It was hot in the city and the buildings were dry from a lack of summer rains. Early planes had dropped 'Blockbuster' bombs which collapsed rubble into the roads. When the fires started, it was almost impossible to reach them. And the reinforcement firemen from Hanover had just left to return to their own city, which too had been struck and left burning.

A firestorm (feuersturm) ignited as fire after fire in Hamburg joined up into one all-consuming blaze. A tornado of fire one thousand feet high rose eerily above the city, generating winds of 170 mph and temperatures exceeding 1,470 °F. It became impossible to breathe as the oxygen was sucked in to feed the firestorm. The asphalt streets quite literally melted, stone glowed red and spilled fuel from stricken tanks poured into the canals, setting them on fire too. The resulting inferno entirely consumed some 8 square miles of the city of Hamburg. German estimates put the death toll at 18,474 - 8,000 of them children.

BELOW: Hamburg after an aerial bombardment during Operation Gomorrha, which started in the night of July 25, 1943, when 791 bombers of the British Royal Air Force (RAF) attacked the city

Many died in their cellars or in public air raid shelters, roasted in the heat or suffocated by carbon monoxide as it replaced the oxygen. Others, caught out on the streets, were sucked up to great heights by the ferocious winds generated by the firestorm and incinerated inside the massive tornado of flame alongside uprooted trees and rooves. A survivor of the horror recalled hearing an unearthly noise *'like an old church organ when someone is playing all the notes at once'*.

'I struggled to run against the wind in the middle of the street... we couldn't go on across (the road} because the asphalt had melted. There were people on the roadway, some already dead, some still lying alive but stuck in the asphalt. They must have rushed on to the roadway without thinking. "Their feet have got stuck and they had put out their hands to try and get out again. They were on their hands and knees screaming.' - Kate Hoffmeister, then 19-years-old.

'Burning horses out of the Hertz hauling business ran past us. The air was burning; simply everything was burning.' - Henni Klank, young mother.

'The blaze was unimaginable. I remember saying to the navigator, who was engrossed with his charts: 'For Christ's sake, Smithy, come and see this. You'll never see the like of it again.' - Flying Officer Trevor Timperley

Miles above, some of the RAF crews swore they could smell the burning flesh, and no-one looked too closely at the ash coating their bombers on return.

ABOVE: Avro Lancaster B Mark II, LL725 'EQ-C', of No. 408 Squadron RCAF, on the ground at Linton-on-Ouse, Yorkshire. Armourers are backing a tractor and trolley loaded with a 4,000 lb HE bomb ('Cookie') and incendiaries under the open bomb-bay. LL725 was lost over Hamburg on 28/29 July 1944

RIGHT: A World War II-era color advertisement, 'Hamburg Knocked Out,' for Emerson Electric showing a birds eye view of a battle ground where you see Hamburg in flames and smoke after an aerial bombing, promoting this Allied power victory is due to the powerfulness of the Emerson Electric motors used in the Allied aircrafts, November 1943. It orginally appeared in 'Aviation, Vol. 42, No. 11,' published by McGraw-Hill Publishing Company

On the night of 29/30 July, the RAF struck Hamburg again with 777 RAF bombers, including 355 Lancasters. Pathfinders using H2S led the attack. The bombers were after the northern suburbs this time, aware that they had been untouched in previous raids. An error in mapping the target however, brought the bombs down short, close to the areas blitzed on 26/27 July. No firestorm was ignited. The RAF lost 28 bombers - 3.6% of the aircraft which took part.

A night raid by 740 bombers was planned for the night of 30/31 July but was mostly called off because of violent thunderstorms over Britain. Despite this, a small number of bombers did actually reach Hamburg, while others diverted to secondary targets. Losses were relatively high. Some 30 aircraft - 4.1% of those taking part - failed to return.

The last Gomorrah raid against Hamburg took place on 3 August 1943, but few of the 740 bombers sent out reached their target due to adverse weather conditions including local thunderstorms. In total 9,000 tons of bombs had been expended on the city. 86 bombers had been lost.

It proved almost impossible to tell how many Germans died during the course of Operation Gomorrah. 37,000 is a widely accepted figure - around 2.4% of the city's total population. Adding to the confusion, most of the bodies recovered were so badly burned as to be unrecognisable. Many of those who had sought shelter in their cellars were cremated where they cowered. In many cases, German authorities were forced to guess how many had died in a particular property by how much ash was found on the floor. Concentration camp inmates were used to clear up the bodies or try to defuse unexploded bombs. The latter details were known as '*Suicide Squads*'.

As the bombing ceased, it's believed that up to a million civilians fled the city, many still in their nightclothes. The workforce available to the Nazis was reduced by at least 10%. 61% of all homes in the city were either destroyed or damaged. About 1/3 of the city's industry was left in ruins and by war's end, most production had not yet been able to reach its pre-Gomorrah capacity.

Behind the scenes, the destruction wrought on Hamburg

ABOVE: Hamburg in ruins

RIGHT: Diagram showing comparison of the Halifax Mk I (pink) with its contemporaries, the Short Stirling (yellow) and the Avro Lancaster (blue)

shook the Nazi High Command. Hitler confided that a few more raids of such intensity and destructive capacity would finish Germany off and they would be forced to sue for peace. Albert Speer concurred, and Josef Goebbels wrote about the *'Sword of Damocles hovering over Germany.'* Among the civilians, there was talking of rising up and sweeping away the Nazis who had brought this upon them. In time, they came to call it *'The November Mood'*. Hitler was asked to visit Hamburg, to help boost morale. He refused. Decades later, Albert Speer admitted that *'Hamburg had suffered the fate Hitler and Goering conceived for London in 1940'*.

In Britain, Gomorrah was considered a triumph. *'Hamburg Smashed!'* thundered the press. For Harris, who admitted that the Gomorrah raids had been *'incomparably more terrible than any previously launched'*, Gomorrah proved that area bombing could have devastating effects on the Nazis and he sought to repeat this with other cities.

Before the war ended, the RAF struck at Hamburg another 69 times…

LANCASTER VS HALIFAX

'The Lancaster is an aeroplane and the Halifax a failure.' - Sir Arthur Harris

Harris loved the Lancaster and little else. It was his *'shining sword'*. He worked hard to get the Stirling bomber cancelled, saying, *'it's murder, plain murder to send my young men out to die in an aircraft like that!'*

Harris was also waging yet another campaign, to have Halifax production ended - even if it meant closing Handley Page. Those in charge there were crooks and incompetents and should be shot. All bomber production, Harris opined, should be switched over to the Lancaster. He presented a plethora of reasons; The Halifax carried far less bombs but put the same number of crew at risk; Lancaster streams had to make dangerous compromises in order to accommodate Halifaxes on joint operations; The Halifax offered lower speeds, lower ceilings and a shorter range. Crews required more training. It was nearly obsolete now and certainly would be by 1944. Halifaxes were more difficult to manufacture - you could build 120 Lancasters for every 100 Halifaxes. Halifax losses per sortie saw 56% more loss than Lancaster sorties. Maintaining a Lancaster was simpler and quicker. And some Halifax crews dismissively referred to their aircraft as *'the Halibag'* or *'fighter bait.'* The Air Staff wouldn't listen. This was a bad time to muck around with production. As a compromise, Harris suggested fitting Lancaster wings onto the Halifax. No-one who mattered was enthused.

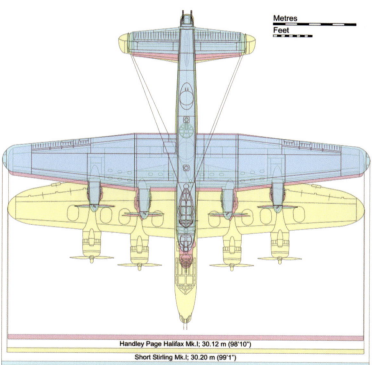

Handley Page Halifax Mk.I; 30.12 m (98'10")
Short Stirling Mk.I; 30.20 m (99'1")
Avro Lancaster Mk.I; 31.09 m (102')

Short Stirling Mk.I; 26.6 m (87'3")
Handley Page Halifax Mk.I; 21.82 m (71'7")
Avro Lancaster Mk.I; 21.18 m (69'5")

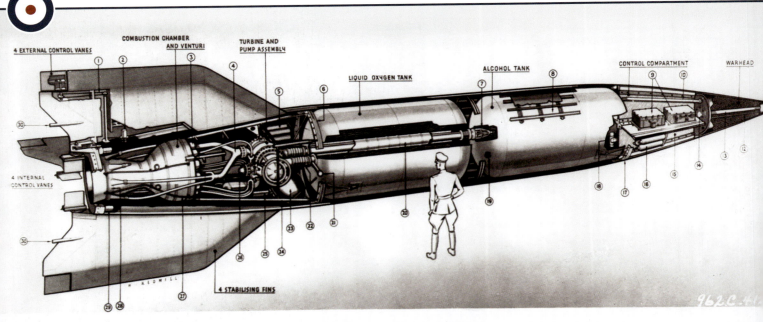

1. CHAIN DRIVE TO EXTERNAL CONTROL VALVE
2. ELECTRIC MOTOR
3. BURNER CUPS
4. ALCHOL SUPPLY FROM PUMP
5. AIR BOTTLES
6. REAR JOINT RING AND STRONG POINT FOR TRANSPORT
7. SERVO-OPERATED ALCOHOL CUTLET VALVE
8. ROCKET SHELL
9. RADIO EQUIPMENT
10. PIPE LEADING FROM ALCOHOL TANK TO WARHEAD
11. NOSE PROBABLY FITTED WITH NOSE SWITCH, OR OTHER DEVICE FOR OPERATING WARHEAD FUZE
12. CONDUIT CARRYING WIRES TO NOSE OF WARHEAD
13. CENTRAL EXPLODER TUBE
14. ELECTRIC FUZE FOR WARHEAD
15. PLYWOOD FRAME
16. NITROGEN BOTTLES
17. FRONT JOINT RING AND STRONG POINT FOR TRANSPORT
18. PITCH AND AZIMUTH GYROS
19. ALOCHOL FILLING POINT
20. DOUBLE WALLED ALCOHOL DELIVERY PIPE TO PUMP
21. OXYGEN FILLING POINT
22. CONCERTINA CONNECTIONS
23. HYDROGEN PEROXIDE TANK
24. TUBULAR FRAME HOLDING TURBINE AND PUMP ASSEMBLY
25. PERMANGANATE TANK (GAS GENERATOR UNIT BEHIND THIS TANK)
26. OXYGEN DISTRIBUTOR FROM PUMP
27. ALCOHOL PIPES FOR SUBSIDIARY COOLING
28. ALCOHOL INLET TO DOUBLE WALL
29. ELECTRO-HYDRAULIC SERVO MOTORS
30. AERIAL LEADS

BATTLE OF THE ROCKET MEN

Germany had developed a secret interest in rocketry ever since the Treaty of Versailles limited their ability to accumulate conventional artillery. Mostly they were interested in a way of delivering gas or high explosives, but there was also some thought given to a Nazi trip to the Moon.

Britain's MI6 knew something about Nazi secret weapons development since almost the start of the war. Their suspicions were supported by the American OSS. Something was happening in Peenemunde, a small island town on the Baltic Sea. There were tantalising photos brought back from Spitfires reconnaissance missions, while intercepted German communications provided further clues. They was talk of something called a V-1 bring developed there, as well as a V-2 and a top secret

ABOVE: A U.S. Army cut-away of the V-2

rocket plane capable of tremendous speeds. If anything, the Allies had too much information. Much was unclear or contradictory. Churchill believed it though. The problem was, Peenemunde was a difficult target. Churchill summed it up by saying:

'Peenemünde is … beyond the range of our radio navigation beams and … we must bomb by moonlight, although the German night fighters will be close at hand and it is too far to send our own. Nevertheless, we must attack it on the heaviest possible scale.'

Furthermore, the complex was widely spread out and protected by smoke screens.

Plans were made.

OPERATION HYDRA

They called it 'Operation Hydra'. On the night of 17/18 August 1943, a 596-strong force from Bomber Command set out to attack the Peenemünde Army Research facility under the command of Group Captain John Searby, CO of 83 Squadron. 324 Lancasters were joined by 218 Halifaxes and 54 Stirlings.

They were out on a killing mission, with the aim of taking out as many Nazi rocket scientists and workers as possible. Destroying the actual facility and the research work therein were regarded as secondary considerations. The crews had not been told the truth about what their target was and instead thought it was a radar development site, but they received a dire warning before they left:

'If the attack fails...it will be repeated the next night and on ensuing nights regardless, within practicable limits, of casualties.' - Order 176.

There was a strong threat of German night fighters en route, so the bomber formation was supported by an elaborate decoy operation. Known as 'Operation Whitebait', it saw eight Pathfinder Mosquitoes from 8 Group despatched to Berlin to drop marker flares, as if the German capital was the bombers' true destination. It worked. Streams of German fighters raced to Berlin to provide cover.

The British bombers arrived over their target relatively unmolested. Their CO played the role of Master Bomber', circling the target, calling down Pathfinder flares and ordering the waves of bombers in. The Stirlings and Halifaxes went in first starting at 00.35 hours. Most target marking went well, assisted by clear skies and bright moonlight. Tragically though, some target indicators had been dropped over the Trassenheide slave labour camp. Almost 500 prisoners were killed by bombs before better-placed flares drew the bombers off to the true target. About 1/3 of the bombers in the first wave actually found and attacked their target, going in at just 7,000 feet before

ABOVE: British plan for the Peenemünde raid

peeling away and turning for home. Although a full three quarters of the Nazi workers housing was successfully destroyed, anti-aircraft shelters were of such quality that only 250 of the 4,000 workers were killed.

In came the second wave, 113 Lancasters with Pathfinder support, with the intent of destroying the rocket facility itself. Their ordnance consisted of almost 100 4,000lb bombs as well as 700 thousand pounders. Unfortunately, the Pathfinders marked their targets with varying degrees of accuracy and strong winds blew flares well off target. As a result a number of Lancasters dropped their bombs on the sea. Some damage was achieved however.

The Third Wave - comprised of 117 Lancasters of 5 Group and 52 Halifax and nine Lancaster bombers of 6 Group - arrived a half an hour after the initial wave had gone in, targeting 70 small buildings which had been judged to be of scientific or storage importance. They arrived to some degree of chaos. Smoke from the previously bombed target was drifting thick over the area and the Germans had got their own smokescreen machines working. Worse, the fighters that

ABOVE: Target 3/Air/389, Attack order with targets highlighted

RIGHT: Ground crews loading and refueling an Avro Lancaster heavy bomber, circa 1943

had earlier been successfully decoyed away to protect Berlin had realised what was really going on and were racing back now to defend Peenemunde - over 200 of them. Despite the chaos, one third of the target buildings were destroyed, including the headquarters building. As the bombers departed, the German night fighters tore into them, taking a fearsome toll. 28 RAF bombers were shot down in just 15 minutes. Another 11 bombers were lost in other actions. Gunners on board the besieged bombers managed to account for five night fighters. In total, the raid cost Bomber Command 6.7% of participants. Those lost were mainly in the Third Wave.

Had the raid worked? Goebbels at the time thought that the rocket project had been delayed for two months but some later historians put the delay at something closer to a maximum of six weeks. Certainly, production moving to the Harz Mountains and tests to Poland would have caused meaningful delays and unexploded bombs going off for several days afterwards at the Peenemunde site caused chaos, as did follow-up raids by USAAF aircraft. Tests of German rockets recommenced on 6 October.

SCHRAGE MUSIK

One of the most deadly weapons that the Luftwaffe could use against Allied bombers was known by the nickname of Schrage Musik or 'Jazz Music'. It was basically a cannon or machine gun mounted on an interceptor that could fire straight upwards. To use it, interceptors had to slip unnoticed directly underneath a target bomber at night. They could then shoot straight up into its fuselage or wing tanks, often with overwhelming destructive force.

The manoeuvre was naturally dangerous for the night fighter pilot as well. There was always the chance of a glancing or full on collision between his aircraft and the intended target bomber. Then there was the distinct possibility that the bomber - especially if was still fully laden - would explode, taking the fighter with it. A further risk was of the interceptor being hit by debris falling off the bomber, or else lethal streams of burning petrol leaking out of its wing tanks. Still, despite this, it was a popular tactic, it usually achieved complete surprise - and it worked. Planes that survived such an attack often put the damage down to flak, and Bomber Command did not have a full grasp of what the Luftwaffe were doing until after the war.

By 1944, over 1/3 of all German night fighters had Schrage Musik installed, usually firing a mixture of armour-piercing, explosive and incendiary ammunition. A two second burst was usually sufficient and on aircraft fitted with 30mm cannon such as some Ju.88s, a single shell might well be enough to bring down the bomber. At the peak of Schrage Musik's deadly effectiveness, Bomber Command began to experience unsustainable losses - and still had little clue what the Germans were doing. Crews and intelligence staff put the casualties down to flak, while aircrew - rattled by Heavies suddenly crumpling in a fireball - bizarrely began to believe that the Germans had developed a 'scarecrow shell' which exploded and only looked like a bomber had been hit.

There was talk of reinstalling the belly gun on the Lancaster as standard. It never happened and, as late

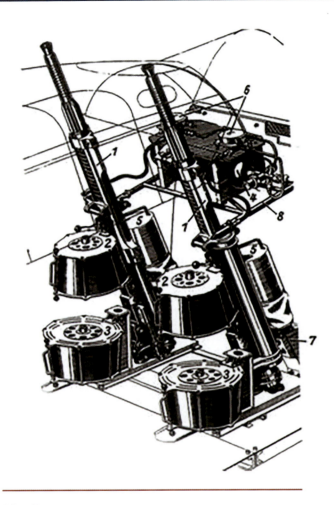

ABOVE: Interior view of Messerschmitt Bf 110G-4 Schräge Musik installation: **1.** MG FF/M **2.** Main drums **3.** Reserve drums **4.** Pressurized container with pressure-reducing gear and stop valve **5.** Spent cases container **6.** FPD and FF (Radio installation) **7.** Weapon mount **8.** Weapon recoil dampener

as 1945, Schrage Musik remained one of the deadliest weapons in the Luftwaffe's arsenal. On 21 February 1945, night fighters fitted with Schrage Musik got in underneath a mass attack by 514 Lancasters headed for the Dortmund-Ems canal. One of Germany's most celebrated fighter aces, Major Heinz-Wolfgang Schnaifer, took just 20 minutes to destroy seven Lancasters using Schrage Musik fitted to his Heinkel He.219. That equated to one bomber every three minutes. That night, it was said that RAF pilots could find their own way home after the raid by simply following the path of Lancasters burning on the ground below.

CHURCHILL'S EAR

The destruction of Hamburg had proved, to Harris's mind at least, that RAF Bomber Command was the mightiest weapon at Britain's disposal. Now he wanted to destroy Berlin - and win the war. There would be no need for a seaborne invasion of occupied Europe, which everyone knew was coming. There would be no need for a grinding, bitter fight by tanks and troops all across the continent. All he had to do was destroy the Nazi capital - the third largest city in the world at the time. The 'Big City' as they called it.

The press were publishing headlines like *'Berlin Next!'* and Germany was desperately strengthening its air defences around the capital. Harris had the number of aircraft he believed he needed - and he had Churchill's ear. Churchill may or may not have liked Harris - but he listened to him. He respected aggressive commanders who thought big, his own instincts nearly always leaned towards offensives and such a grand strike would at least ease Stalin's incessant demands for the West to open a Second Front. Harris was a regular weekend guest at the Prime Minister's country residence, Chequers - which was close by to Bomber Command HQ at High Wycombe - and this gave him access to the very top in a way that made many of his superiors peevish and jealous.

Harris said he was certain that he could *'push Germany over'* by the end of 1943 with sufficient bombing - and made the mistake of telling others that. In their eyes he had now made a promise to win the war for them. In November 1943, Harris put it in writing to Churchill.

> **'We can wreck Berlin from end to end if the USAAF come in with us. It will cost us between 400 and 500 aircraft. It will cost Germany the war.'**

'The Mighty 8th' did not come in with them. They had suffered devastating losses amounting to some 20% on their recent daylight raids and US commanders were far more interested in landing boots on French beaches. They implored the Air Ministry to take Harris aside and make him concentrate on bombing aircraft production plants instead.

So Harris went it alone.

THE WILD BOARS

Window was still playing havoc with German fighter defences. Ground stations could no longer vector interceptors onto targets with any degree of confidence and the fighters' on-board radar was equally unreliable. As a necessity, the Germans changed tactics to something they called 'Wild Boar.'

Now, fighters would be scrambled directly over the target area and go hunting for RAF aircraft as they commenced their bombing runs. Since they couldn't rely on radar, they would have to rely on their eyes to see a bomber. It might be silhouetted against a burning city or perhaps caught in the searchlights. Ground defences shot up flares to try and further illuminate enemy aircraft. If they saw one, their orders were to close in, dodging in and out of the flak, and kill it.

ABOVE: 'The Wild Boars' - "Wilde Sau" emblem

FALSE CHEER

By October 1943 Bomber Command could boast 30 front line Lancaster squadrons. By New Year it was expected to be 40. Harris could rely on 160 new Lancasters turning up every month. Harris had scorched and pulverised Hamburg. Now he wanted to do the same to Berlin. The public were enthused. The Daily Mirror spoke of '*emasculation*'.

It is said that when RAF aircrew heard that their next target was to be Berlin, there were hearty cheers from amongst the ranks. Deep down however, the aircrew knew that Berlin was a daunting target. It was far to the East of the nation, which meant longer missions and more chances of things going wrong. It had the best defences in the entire Reich - thick searchlight coverage over 60 miles across which made one RAF crewman joke that, as they made their bombing run, it felt like '*running naked through a busy railway station*',

40 miles of anti-aircraft guns including three truly gigantic flak towers bristling with 24 128-mm anti-aircraft guns grouped in eight-gun batteries and night fighters buzzing like flies over the city. The buildings were generally built better than those in Hamburg, which probably meant more missions were needed to destroy the city - all 883 square miles of it.

LEFT: 12.8-cm-Flak on a flak tower

BELOW: A member of the ground crew, illuminated by a lamp shining from the bomb-aimer's position, guides Avro Lancaster B Mark III, JB362 'EA-D', ('D for Donald') of No. 49 Squadron RAF to its dispersal point at Fiskerton, Lincolnshire, after returning from the greatest and most destructive raid mounted on Berlin to date (22/23 November 1943); the main weight of the raid falling in the centre and south of the city with extensive damage both to housing and to industrial premises. Warrant Officer H Blunt and his crew arrived safely back at their dispersal a few minutes before midnight on 22 November, but were shot down and killed in 'D for Donald' when returning from their next visit to Berlin, Germany on 27 November 1943

OFF TO THE BIG CITY –
THE BATTLE OF BERLIN

'Hell seems to have broken loose over us…' - Josef Goebbels

'This is a calculated, remorseless campaign of destruction…' - Ed Murrow, broadcaster

'What we want to do, in addition to the horrors of fire, is to bring masonry crashing down on top of the Boche, to kill the Boche and to terrify the Boche.' - Arthur Harris

Harris's grand assault on the German capital began rather inauspiciously. On 18/19 November, 416 Lancasters, with 4 Mosquito Pathfinders, were despatched to attack Berlin using H2S. A further 395 aircraft flew on diversionary raids. However, there was relatively heavy cloud over the target and little was achieved. The raid killed 143 Berliners and made 7,326 homeless. Bomber Command lost a total of 32 aircraft - nine of them conducting the main raid.

More successful was the raid on the night of 22/23 November flown by 469 Lancasters, 234 Halifaxes, 50 Stirlings and 11 Mosquitoes, which severely damaged homes to the west of the city centre. They dropped over 2,500 tons of bombs and incendiaries in a raid lasting little more than half an hour. No capital city in the world had ever been hit so hard in the history of aerial warfare. The raid also ignited several firestorms - but nothing on a scale that could be compared to Hamburg. 2,000 Berliners were killed and a further 175,000 made homeless. The famous KaDeWe department store was obliterated by a stricken British bomber which crashed squarely on its roof. Albert Speer lost his personal office and his ministry building - and Adolf Hitler's private train was wrecked. The Neukölln Gasworks exploded. Bomber Command lost 26 aircraft - 3.4 per cent of the force despatched. The next night that of 23/24 November 1943 saw Berlin hit again by 365 Lancasters, 10 Halifaxes and eight Mosquitoes. 1,000 Berliners were killed and a further 100,000 made homeless.

On the night of 26/27 November Berlin was again attacked this time by 443 Lancasters and seven Mosquitoes. Confusion over laying Window accurately led to 21 heavy bombers being brought down by withering anti-aircraft fire over the target. The city centre was struck, along with industrial areas. Simultaneously, another bomber force comprised mainly of Halifaxes hit Stuttgart. Total losses for both missions amounted to 34 bombers - a painful 5.1%. Heavy fog over the home airfields helped cause many landing accidents and inflated the figure.

Bad casualty figures for the Stirling bomber saw it withdrawn from all Berlin operations quite quickly. With a maximum ceiling of 16,500ft, it was relatively easy prey. Most of the Halifaxes went just a scant few weeks later.

On the night of 2/3 December, Bomber Command received more heavy losses over Berlin. 425 Lancasters, 18 Mosquitoes and 15 Halifaxes were sent on the raid. Heavy cross-winds helped to scatter the bomber stream, and the Germans correctly identified the destination of the incoming bomber force, enabling them to put up a particularly powerful Wild Boar response. The night fighters tore into the raiders and shot down 40 of them, 37 of which were Lancasters. Most of the bombs fell considerably south of their target, but there was some notable damage caused to Berlin's railways and two major industrial targets.

The next sizeable raid on Berlin came on the night of 16/17 December, with 483 Lancasters and 15 Mosquitoes taking part. 25 Lancasters were destroyed during the raid, but another 29 were lost struggling to land back home in England due to fog and low cloud. They called it *'Black Thursday.'* Over three hundred airmen died. The raid did however succeed in causing major damage to Berlin's rail network and by now, the cumulative effect of the raids had made 25% of all homes in Berlin uninhabitable.

364 Lancasters, 8 Mosquitoes and 7 Halifaxes made the run to Berlin once again on the night of 23/24 December. Bad weather made operations difficult for both the bomber crews and the German interceptors. 16 Lancasters were lost but bombing damage was relatively light. The last significant bombing raid of 1943 on Berlin came on 29/30 December. 457 Lancasters, 252 Halifaxes and 3 Mosquitos struck at the city but with little success because of heavy cloud cover. Losses too were light - just 2.8% - as the Wild Boars found it difficult to find the bombers amidst the clouds.

1943 came to an end and eyebrows were being raised in certain quarters. Despite persistent strikes Berlin was far from destroyed and the Nazis showed no signs of suing for peace. Harris though he knew what to do: Keep going and hit them harder still in 1944.

RIGHT: 'Two Bus loads over Berlin' - 1943 poster

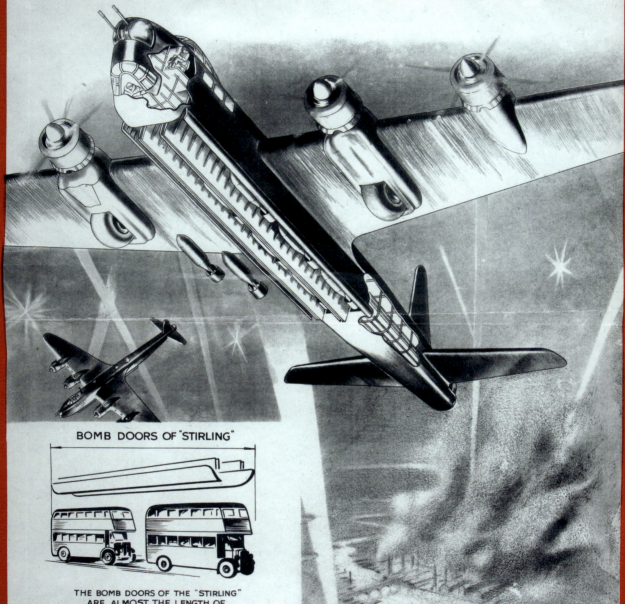

'I've been trying to hit Cologne Cathedral for years.'
Arthur Harris

TIME IS WASTING

It was an open secret: 1944 was the year in which the Allies would finally launch the invasion of Europe. No-one knew where, but it was obvious that D-Day would have to come in the summer of the year, because of the sheer difficulty of getting troops safely over the Channel in poor weather.

Harris understood this, and he also knew that, when the time came, he would be expected to put Bomber Command at the disposal of the invasion planners. If he was to win the war, and thus make invasion unnecessary, he had a few scant months at best to pulverise the Nazis and Berlin into submission.

BACK TO BERLIN

In reality, the 'Battle of Berlin' had never stopped. It had just taken on a new urgency.

On 1st January, 421 Lancasters made the long trip out to Berlin again. Diversionary raids on other targets failed to draw the night fighters away and, as a result, 6.7% of the Lancasters were lost. It was a chilling start for what was becoming another grinding war of attrition. 362 Lancasters returned on the next night and, in a blazing battle over the target area itself, 27 more Lancasters were lost.

Bomber Command would not return in force until the night of 20/21 January when 495 Lancasters along with 264 Halifaxes and 10 Mosquitoes attacked Berlin. Losses amounted to 4.6% of the force - 22 Halifaxes and 13 Lancasters.

Returning on the night of 27/28 January, 515 Lancasters and 15 Mosquitos bombed the city over a wide and scattered area. Diversionary raids did successfully draw off some of the night fighters, but Bomber Command still lost 33 Lancasters that night. Lancasters targeted Berlin the following night - 432 of them - together with 242 Halifaxes and 4 Mosquitoes. They launched a heavily concentrated attack on the southern and western parts of the city, but losses were again severe. 46 bombers were shot down, meaning a casualty rate of 6.8%. Percentage losses were only slightly lower the following night, when 440 Lancasters, 82 Halifaxes and a dozen Mosquitoes reappeared over Berlin. 33 bombers were lost on the raid this time, an attrition rate of 6.2%. Something was going to have to give soon…

Bomber Command paused and drew breath, but they were back striking Berlin again by the night of 14/15 February in what was to be the largest attack on Germany's capital of

RIGHT: Colourised image, Cologne Cathedral stands seemingly undamaged (although having been directly hit several times and damaged severely) while entire area surrounding it is completely devastated

the entire war. 561 Lancasters were joined by 314 Halifaxes and 16 Mosquitoes. Conducted with such overwhelming force, the raid successfully smashed many of the city's industrial plants with tons of HE and incendiaries raining down on Siemensstadt, the centre and south-western districts of the city. A decoy run by 24 Lancasters pretending to be destined for Hamburg failed to fool Berlin's night fighter defences. The bombers were hit hard by enemy interceptors and 43 were shot down, of which 26 were Lancasters and 17 Halifaxes. Worse was to follow. On the night of 24/25 March, a large scale bombing raid on Berlin became scattered and bombed targets well south of the city. Night fighters tore into them and 72 bombers were lost - a clearly unsustainable percentage loss rate of 8.9%.

The Battle for Berlin was now effectively over. RAF Bomber Command would avoid the city for much of the remainder of 1944.

NUREMBERG

Bomber Command got another appalling shock on the night of 30/31 March 1944, when Nuremberg was attacked by 572 Lancasters, 214 Halifaxes and 9 Mosquitoes (795 aircraft). They had been intended for Berlin, but diverted because of weather conditions. As the bomber stream came in, the Germans correctly guessed their target destination and despatched hordes of night fighters which smashed into the bomber streams at the Belgian border. 82 bombers were successfully shot down between the border and Nuremberg and a further 13 brought down limping for home. With a loss rate of 11.9%, it was the costliest Bomber Command raid of the war. Harris admitted it was '*the one real disaster*' of his time in command.

PREPARING FOR D-DAY

Harris was not yet ready to give up on bombing Berlin into submission, but those above him were. He had expended vast resources for six months and there was no sign of the Nazis surrendering. The invasion of Europe now took priority. Bomber Command was placed directly under the control of the man who would command the invasion - General Dwight D. Eisenhower - on April 14, 1944. Harris understood it as an *'inescapable commitment'*, but also worried that it would often mean bombing in daylight. His forces were used to the night.

From March onwards, Bomber Command began following the Zuckermann or 'Transport' Plan, They were instructed to destroy rail and road transport links, not just in the Normandy area but also numerous decoy targets as well as Western Germany. The aim was to prevent the Germans from being able to move men, weaponry and supplies around in response to Allied moves. Experimental raids began in March 1944, and no-one was more surprised than Harris at how well Bomber Command adapted to the task. By June 5, it was recorded that Bomber Command had dropped 45,000 tons of bombs on thirty-seven different railways. 22 railway targets were *'sufficiently damaged to require no more attention'* and a further 15 were believed to b*e 'severely damaged.'*. Rail connections between France and Germany were described a*s 'severely crippled.'*

During the spring of 1944, Bomber Command's frontline strength was 1,360 aircraft so, whenever the force was not fully extended hitting tactical targets, Harris sneaked in a quick raid on a German city. 846 bombers set off for Frankfurt on the night of 18 March. Almost 100 industrial sites were destroyed, 55,000 civilians rendered homeless and 43 aircraft lost. Great swathes of the city were burned and left in ruins.

As D-Day grew closer, from early May onwards the priority switched to attacking coastal gun emplacements, radar stations, ammo dumps and any massed troops or armour. Bomber Command expended 7,000 tons of

ABOVE: Avro Lincoln BII Bomb Bay

bombs against the batteries in May, destroying five in Normandy and, it was believed, crippling a further six. On the night of 5/6 June, on the very eve of the invasion, Bomber Command put up a force of very nearly 1,000 planes - 551 of them Lancasters - to attack the big coastal batteries. The Luftwaffe was taken completely by surprise and could only muster a feeble effort to attack the massed bomber waves, but unfortunately the weather was bad and, despite dropping a record payload of 4,500 tons of ordnance on the emplacements, success was mixed at best. Only three bombers were lost in the raid. Meanwhile No.617 Lancasters dropped Window off Calais to simulate a dummy invasion fleet. In the week following D-Day, Bomber Command dutifully flew 3,500 sorties in support of the invasion and dropped 11,800 tons of bombs on transport links still capable of being used by the Germans. By now, the Luftwaffe was losing five hundred aircraft a week. Correspondingly, Bomber Commands losses on an average raid dropped to 1%. During June, July and August, V-1 flying bombs - the fruits of Peenemunde - began to fall on London and southern England. Both the USAAF and Bomber Command were charged with going after their

ABOVE: The Navigational Officer of No. 83 Squadron RAF points out the course of a bombing raid to Bremen on a large map in the Briefing Room at Scampton, Lincolnshire

launch sites and storage facilities, but with only a degree of success. Better home defences eventually solved the problem of '*those damn silly rockets*', as Harris called them.

THE AVRO LINCOLN

The Avro Lincoln was intended to supersede the Lancaster. Originally it was thought of as an actual Lancaster and prototypes were officially designated the Lancaster IV and V. These were renamed the Lincoln I and II.

The Lincoln was an improvement on the existing Lancaster design and was developed by Roy Chadwick himself. The new aircraft was more robust and the fuselage larger than previous Lancasters, enabling it to carry up to 11 tons of bombs as well as extra fuel and giving it a new maximum range of 4,450 miles. The operational ceiling of the Lincoln was 35,000 feet and it was capable of a maximum speed of 310 mph. It was fitted with four two-stage supercharged Rolls-Royce Merlin 85 engines.

The first prototype had its maiden flight on 9 June 1944 at Ringway Airport and it was given operational status in August 1945, too late to see action in Europe. It was intended to form part of 'Tiger Force' in the Far East, but the surrender of Japan prevented this. It did however later see action during the Mau-Mau rebellion in Kenya and the emergency in Malaya. Almost 600 Lincolns were built, serving with 29 RAF Squadrons. It continued to serve with the RAF until 1963.

TARGET GERMANY

While Harris obeyed his instructions to support the invasion, he was also on occasions in possession of enough resources to go after his favourite targets - the cities of Nazi Germany. He intended to be relentless. And he was relentless.

On 18 August a night raid by 274 Lancasters, Halifaxes and Mosquitoes devastated the centre of Bremen. The fires started by incendiaries quickly spread to the northern suburbs and the port facilities. Over 1,000 bodies were found in the aftermath. Many had been asphyxiated or else roasted in their cellars or the public shelters. Another 375 were reported missing and were never found. Almost 9,000 homes were rendered useless and eighteen ships were sunk in the port. Only one aircraft, a Lancaster was lost on the raid. It was Stettin's turn eleven nights later. Just over 400 Lancasters destroyed 55 factory facilities and sank 2,000 tons of shipping. This time casualties were relatively heavy, with 22 Lancasters accounted for by night fighters and anti-aircraft guns.

MAIN IMAGE: An RAF officer inspects the hole left by a 22,000-lb deep-penetration 'Grand Slam' bomb which pierced the reinforced concrete roof of the German submarine pens at Farge, north of Bremen, Germany. this was the result of a daylight raid mounted by 18 Avro Lancasters of No. 617 Squadron RAF

LEFT: 15-foot reinforced ferro-concrete U-Boat pen roof penetrated by a 22,000 lb MC Grand Slam bomb

DARMSTADT

The raid on Darmstadt on 11 September almost wiped the city clean off the map. Sirens sounded in Darmstadt just after 11.30pm and as families fled down to their cellars what little defences the city had in terms of AA guns and searchlights swung into action. Lured to the city by important railway links and well on their way now were 226 Lancasters and 14 Halifaxes and Mosquitoes, packed with 4,000lb HE bombs and the maximum possible number of incendiaries. There was another reason Darmstadt was chosen. By now, Bomber command had inflicted such damage on larger and more important German cities so that they were *'no longer worth bombing.'*

The first Pathfinder flares fell at 11.45pm, lighting up the while of the west of the city bright crimson. Back up flares from 83 and 97 Squadrons painted the sky green. Then - at 11.57 - the bomber force was ordered to commence. All hell broke loose in the city centre, igniting fires that rapidly spread to southern and eastern suburbs. Every building seemed to crack, crumble and burn. In cellars, temperatures quickly reached unbearable levels and

families were forced to flee out onto the fiery streets. *'Burning people raced past like live torches,'* reported one survivor, *'and I listened to their unforgettable final screams.'* In another part of the city a graveyard received a direct hit from a 400lb bomb, disinterring the corpses and throwing them high in the air.

The raid lasted for 51 minutes and cost 12 Lancasters. On the ground, over 12,000 people were reported dead. 70,000 were made homeless in a city that now barely existed.

BELOW: Two American soldiers stand behind a fence and survey the damage sustained during a saturation bombing raid on the city of Darmstadt, Germany, 1945. The raid, conducted on September 11 & 12, 1944 by British Royal Air Force Bomber Command, resulted in thousands of deaths, and rendered more than half the city's inhatants homeless

FREEDOM

Bomber Command remained under the control of Eisenhower until September 1944, clocking up some 24,600 sorties in support of the Normandy invasion. Eisenhower showered Harris with praise for his co-operation and turned him loose. Even though Harris was free of Eisenhower, he was still under the control of the Air Staff and in short order they gave him commands to prioritise attacks on oil-related targets, transport hubs and enemy armour. Harris bristled and complained; in response he got another directive only reinforcing the Air Staff's wishes. In response, Harris scribbled *'Here we go round the mulberry bush - ATH'* on the top of the directive and shoved it to one side. He did obey but only to an extent, just so he had something he could point to if his missions were questioned. In reality, less than 6% of Bomber Commands sorties were flown against oil-related targets in the last two months of 1944. Harris still believed that only the wholesale destruction of German cities could end the war. Still, when he could sneak way to ravage German cities, he found that average losses had dropped to just 2 %. Why? Germany's lack of Pilots. Lack of Planes. Lack of fuel. Lack of guns. Lack of everything. For example, in April 1944, Germany was producing 175,000 tons of aviation fuel every month. By September 1944, that figure had slumped to just 7,000 tons. Harris on the other hand now had 1,400 heavy bombers available to him every single day. There were 51 operational Lancaster Squadrons. It was a force so powerful that everyone from Churchill down didn't really know what to do with it. But Harris did. Eventually his bosses decided on disrupting fuel supplies, but Harris was too wilful to fully comply. *'We should now get on and knock Germany flat,'* he told Churchill.

MAIN IMAGE: A Lancaster III of No 619 Squadron, based at Coningsby, 14 February 1944

BELOW: Major General Dwight Eisenhower.

1944

115

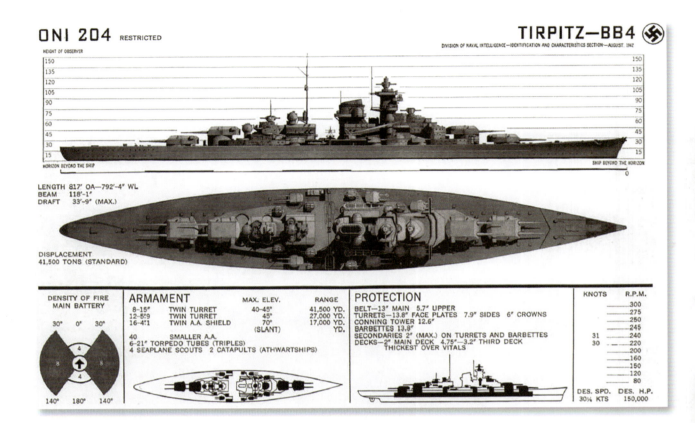

TARGET TIRPITZ

'The lonely queen of the north'.

Winston Churchill called her *'The Beast.'*

At more than 53,500 tonnes *the Tirpitz* was the heaviest battleship ever built by a European power. Launched in 1939, her main battery consisted of four turrets each containing two 15 inch guns with a range of over 22 miles. She packed over 100 smaller guns, and after 1942, was retrofitted with torpedo tubes. Her defensive armour was as thick as 14 inches in critical areas and in speed trials she proved capable of exceeding 35 mph. Her crew amounted to some 108 officers and 2,500 men.

Stationed in the far north to dominate the Baltic, she posed a severe threat to Soviet warships and Allied aid convoys into Russia. Her very presence tied up considerable amounts of Royal Navy warships, just in case she might try to break out into the North Sea or the Channel. The occupied Norwegians contemptuously referred to her as

In late 1943, while in Northern Norway, the *Tirpitz* was attacked by three Royal Navy midget submarines and severely damaged by charges from the craft. Fuel tanks were ruptured, almost 12,500 tons of water flooded the warship and one of her turrets was dislocated and could no longer rotate. Repairs were not completed until April 1944. While she was laid up, there were frequent bombing missions conducted by carrier-based aircraft of the Fleet Air Arm without any significant effect. The job of sinking the *Tirpitz* was then passed on to Bomber Command and No.5 Group in particular. The *Tirpitz* was now Hitler's last great battleship.

ABOVE: Recognition drawing prepared by the US Navy

The first attack - Operation Paravane - came on 15 September 1944, when a force of 23 Lancasters from 9 and 617 Squadrons left their special forward operating base in Russia for Norway. 17 carried one 'Tallboy' bomb each and the further six carried twelve experimental JW mines. (Crews were told not to return to base with mines under any circumstance. They were all rigged to explode after 15 hours). *Tirpitz's* on-board radar failed to detect them coming as they were shielded by mountains. Only one of the Tallboys struck the battleship as it sat nestled under a cliff in Kaa Fjord but it was enough to cause significant damage. Landing near the bow, the Tallboy ripped through the ship's armour and exited through the bottom before exploding on the floor of the Fjord. 2,000 tons of water rushed in to forward compartments and the shock of the explosion wrecked the ship's fire control system and limited her speed to 10mph at best. Some hull plates and bulkheads were also buckled. In October, she limped out of the fjord and made her way to another fjord further south near Tromso which would hopefully be safer. All the Lancasters made it safely back, except for one which was forced to crash-land.

ABOVE: Bomber command load one of the new 12,000 pound "earthquake" bombs onto a Lancaster II bomber, the same bombs that sunk the 45,000 ton German battleship Tirpitz in Norway. 14th October 1944

Nos.9 and 617 Squadrons went after her again with a high level raid on 29 October. This time, Operation Obviate saw 32 Lancasters taking part in the raid, each outbound from Lossiemouth in Scotland and armed with a Tallboy. Many

ABOVE: Tirpitz under attack by British carrier aircraft on 3 April 1944

of the Lancasters were forced to make multiple runs at the ship before being satisfied enough to drop their ordnance - but still all the bombs missed the Tirpitz, partly as a result of poor visibility over the target. One Lancaster was damaged by shore-based anti-aircraft batteries. Crews received a message on returning home from No.5 Group's commander, Air Commodore Ralph Cochrane.

'Congratulations on your splendid flight and perseverance. Luck won't always favour the Tirpitz. One day you'll get her.'

Cochrane meant what he said. Crews were told in no uncertain terms that they would be ordered to return time and again if necessary until 'The Beast' was sunk.

09.35 on the morning of 12 November 1944 saw the launch of Operation Catechism. Again 9 and 617 squadrons were assigned the task and 32 Lancasters took part, 27 of them armed with 'Tallboys', flying from the North of Scotland with extra fuel tanks. The *Tirpitz* was now better defended than she had been before, with additional anti-aircraft guns positioned on either side of the Fjord and anti-torpedo nets slung underneath her. Two anti-aircraft flak ships were stationed in close proximity and smoke generators were in the process of being installed. 38 Luftwaffe fighters were stationed within reach to give powerful air cover against raiders.

617 Squadron led the attack in near-perfect weather, followed by No.9 Squadron. 617 Squadron's commanding officer, Wing Commander 'Willie' Tait, spotted the Tirpitz from about 20 miles out. He reported that the battleship

was *'lying squat and black among her torpedo nets like a spider in her web, silhouetted against the glittering blue and green waters of the fjord.'*

As the bombers came in at 14-15,000 feet, fierce fire from the *Tirpitz*'s 15cm secondary guns caused the Lancasters to break formation temporarily, but they persisted in their attack. Luftwaffe fighters charged with protecting the moored and vulnerable ship were not alerted and so did not take off.

One Tallboy struck the ship squarely between its main A and B turrets but unaccountably failed to explode. A second Tallboy, dropped by Wing Commander Tait, hit the *Tirpitz* amidships between her aircraft catapult and a funnel. This bomb exploded with full force, tearing great jagged holes in the battleship's side and bottom. A mix of pressurised steam and smoke spurted 300 feet into the air. The 824 foot-long ship began to tremble from stem to stern and then started to list. Within ten minutes, the ship was listing at close to 40 degrees and her captain gave the order to abandon ship. Many of the crew jumped into the water and started to swim for shore. Eight minutes later for reasons never fully understood the *Tirpitz*'s main C turret exploded with such force that a large chunk of the turret was thrown over 80 feet into the air. It came down amongst the sailors desperately swimming for shore, crushing many of them. The great battleship then rolled over and firmly lodged itself in the bed of the Fjord. No Lancasters were lost on the raid, but one Lancaster from No.9 Squadron was damaged by shore-based batteries and was forced to make an emergency landing in neutral Sweden.

Such was the shock and confusion caused that no-one really knows how many German sailors died when the *Tirpitz* sank. Some estimates put the figure as high as 1200 men out of a reduced compliment of 1600 that the ship had been operating with. All the senior officers died. 82 men trapped in the upturned hull of the battleship were known to have been rescued by cutting through the plating on the ship's underside as desperate calls went out for acetylene torches. It's said that any local Norwegians who possessed one quickly hid it. Some even started to celebrate at the water's edge, whereupon they were swiftly arrested by the Gestapo.

Back home in Britain, the men who took part were personally congratulated by Winston Churchill, members of his war cabinet and even King George VI. Many were decorated. Wing Commander Tait was recommended for a Victoria Cross but the request got buried in bureaucracy and he never received it.

Parts of the *Tirpitz's* armoured plating is still used by local councils near the Fjord to temporarily cover up any potholes in their roads.

TOWARDS VICTORY

Harris sensed victory now, and he went for it. During October, Bomber Command Lancasters just rolled over major German cities. Cologne, Hanover, Nuremberg and Stuttgart were all hammered - with a loss rate of just 1%. At the end of the month, 771 Heavies struck Essen, completely devastating the Krupps pig-iron plant. Possibly as a sop to his betters, Harris did turn his attention to oil-related targets throughout November, launching 22 major strikes. Such was his confidence now - and the battered state of Germany's defences - that he chose to conduct 14 of these attacks during daylight. It is shocking to contemplate that of all the bombs dropped by the RAF during the entire war, 46% of them would be dropped in the final nine months. Some cities still possessed strategic importance. But others - like Bonn, Magdeburg and Freiberg with nothing to recommend them as targets - were also attacked. 4,000 civilians died in a firestorm in Magdeburg. Another firestorm in little Pforzheim killed 17,600 - a quarter of the entire population. Pforzheim produced clocks. Cities that had already been reduced to wastelands were bombed again. And again. Thousands of years of European culture would be pulverised. When the American legend Jimmy Doolittle apologised for accidentally bombing Strasbourg Cathedral, Harris just laughed, congratulated him and said,' *I've been trying to hit Cologne Cathedral for years.'*

BELOW: The crew of an RAF Lancaster bomber discuss their flight before take-off from an airfield in East Anglia, 15th September 1944

> '**I do not personally regard the whole of the remaining cities of Germany as worth the bones of one British Grenadier.**'
>
> Sir Arthur Harris

ALMOST THERE

As 1945 came in, there was no doubt whatsoever who was going to win the war. By February, Soviet forces were less than ten miles from Berlin.

At this time, Winston Churchill was feeling alarmed. The triumvirate which had been directing the war effort to date - himself, Roosevelt and Stalin - was starting to feel more like a duo with Churchill being progressively pushed aside. Churchill keenly understood who Stalin was - nothing more than a brutal, ignorant thug - but Roosevelt seemed to think otherwise. Churchill suspected that the two men were planning in secret on how they might divide the world up between themselves in the post war years. Churchill started to make plans to fight the Soviet Union if need be, but at the same time realised he needed to show Roosevelt and Stalin that he was still a force to be reckoned with. His most powerful weapon was Bomber Command. With his bombers deployed, Churchill saw a chance to demonstrate British might to the Soviets, saying '*Berlin, and no doubt other large cities in Eastern Germany should now be considered especially attractive targets.*' When planning seemed to flag, it was Churchill who kept it moving and would bristle at any delays.

ABOVE RIGHT: Portraits of Churchill and Stalin

OPERATION THUNDERCLAP - DRESDEN

'*The attack on Dresden was at the time considered a military necessity by much more important people than myself.*' - Sir Arthur Harris.

Dresden was the largest German city not to have received a raid of any significance but it was a legitimate target. It was a major communications centre, railway hub and home to 110 factories all contributing to the war effort.

Harris had doubts about attacking Dresden, the state capital of Saxony, not because of the possibility of heavy civilian casualties or because its place at the centre of European heritage (It had long been known as '*The*

BEYOND

German Florence') but because of the dangers its posed to his bomber crews. No one knew much about how strong the city's defences might be and the distance to the target was long and arduous. Crews might be expected to be in the air for a round trip of some ten hours duration, all the while in potentially dangerous winter weather. Bomber Command didn't even possess proper maps of the place. There were better targets, he said, but higher hearts and minds were set on Dresden.

The American 8th were scheduled to strike the very first blow against Dresden on the morning of 13 February, but they couldn't take off from their British bases because of heavy rain so it was left to Bomber Command to land the first bombs. No.5 Group bombers - codenamed 'Plate Rack' - would hit the city first at 10.15pm, with each bomber carrying a 4,000lb HE Cookie as well as 8,000lbs of incendiaries. A much larger force comprised of Heavies from 1, 3, 6 and 8 Groups would come in some three hours later, intentionally catching and killing emergency workers as they struggled to help victims of the earlier raid.

ABOVE: 57 Squadron Avro Lancaster with the "Usual" area bombing load of a 4,000 lb (1.8 t) bomb and 12 Small Bomb Containers, each filled with 4 lb (1.8 kg) incendiary bombs

244 Lancasters in the first wave started taking off at around 6pm on the start of an epic 900 mile outbound journey to Dresden. They swept over the French Coast at 220mph, staying south to avoid the still-formidable air defences of the Ruhr.

By ten to ten at night, the German authorities had realised that Dresden was the target, and air raid sirens sounded in the city. Within half an hour, parts of the sky were lit up green and white by Pathfinder target indicators. The Germans had nicknamed them *'Christmas Trees'*. They were joined minutes later by a fresh batch of crimson target indicators dropped from Mosquitoes haring across the city at 3,000 feet. Above, the waiting Heavies received the instruction *'Attack Red T.I's as planned'*. The first 14 bombers began to descend to cloud level at 8,000 feet to commence their bombing runs. All hit their targets and the next Lancasters coming in could already see numerous fierce fires amidst the T.Is. 17 more Lancasters came in, this time from 49 Squadron bombing at altitudes ranging from 12-14,000 feet. Now huge explosions seemed to rock the city. The raid last 15 minutes and left a city so deep in flames that the glow could be seen 100 miles away.

Below, the entire city centre was in flames. People clung together in the shelters as above them buildings crumbled and streets heaved and ripped apart. Flames started gathering force, leaping from building to building. Some people tried to run, covering themselves in wet blankets for protection. Blazing rubble fell on them, pinning them down in the flames to die. Some people simply disintegrated while others choked and suffocated underground. Dresden's fire services were completely overwhelmed within just minutes. The streets were blocked and impassable. Raging flames leapt a mile into the air while black smoke rose to 15,000 feet over the city.

And it was just the beginning. Dresden had had very little to defended itself with. Its last large flak battery had been removed from the city in January to be used on the Russian Front, and the Luftwaffe by now had few pilots and little fuel. There was also a severe lack of adequate public shelters and the population was swollen with

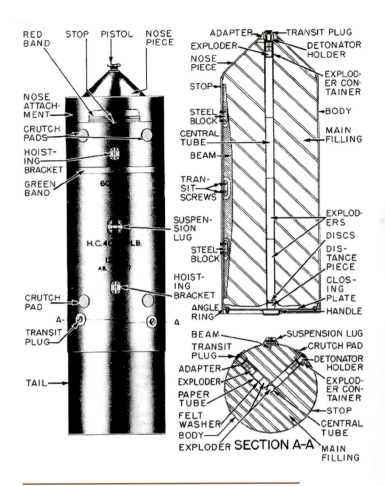

ABOVE: Diagram of a 4,000-lb HC Mark I bomb

refugees trying to escape the advancing Russians.

550 more Bomber Command aircraft were now well on their way, having taken off from the airfields in England by 10pm. They came in a giant stream that stretched for over 120 miles in the German night skies. Air raid sirens sounded again at just gone one in the morning - those that could be hand-cranked now that the electricity was out - and quarter of an hour later the bombers arrived. The 60 Pathfinders of 8 Group hardly needed to drop their T.Is. Much of the city was alight below them. Instead they just dumped their flares into the conflagration and headed home again.

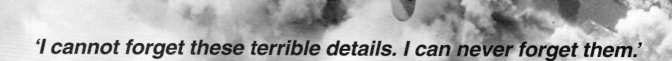

'I cannot forget these terrible details. I can never forget them.'

Lothar Metzger

As the bombers circled above waiting their turn, the firestorm raged below, Roads melted. People were simply sucked up into the mile-high firestorm by irresistible winds and flash-cremated alive in seconds. Members of the emergency services, struggling to help survivors, choked to death on the red-hot ash and cinders filling the air. Families roasted to death as shelters became ovens.

'We saw terrible things: cremated adults shrunk to the size of small children, pieces of arms and legs, dead people, whole families burnt to death, burning people ran to and fro, burnt coaches filled with civilian refugees, dead rescuers and soldiers, many were calling and looking for their children and families, and fire everywhere, everywhere fire, and all the time the hot wind of the firestorm threw people back into the burning houses they were trying to escape from.

'To my left I suddenly see a woman. I can see her to this day and shall never forget it. She carries a bundle in her arms. It is a baby. She runs, she falls, and the child flies in an arc into the fire… Insane fear grips me and from then on I repeat one simple sentence to myself continuously: "I don't want to burn to death". I do not know how many people I fell over. I know only one thing: that I must not burn.' –Margaret Freyer

The second raid lasted for 23 minutes. When it was over and the last Lancasters were on their way home, Dresden could now be seen burning from 200 miles away. And the 'Mighty 8th' were just starting their engines back in England. In total six British bombers were lost on the raids, three of them after being hit by a friendly bomber directly above them dropping its ordnance on top of them.

The firestorm had mostly extinguished itself when, at noon on February 14th, 311 Flying Fortresses appeared over what was left of Dresden, but a thousand smaller fires still burned amidst the smoke and rubble (There was meant to be 400 but some had got lost and ended up bombing Prague). A 13 minute raid by the 8th resulted in 136,800 incendiary bombs and 2,000 500lb bombs dropping on the city. There was little enough intact down below to make much difference now. The following day 210 Fortresses came back to the city to make sure its railway yards were destroyed.

Crews headed home joking about breaking all the china in Dresden. At home, the press celebrated. *'Smashing blows against Dresden,'* thundered the Times, while the Daily Express proposed a new verb - *'to Dresden'* something.

Below German propaganda insisted that 400,000 people had died in the horror. Today, that figure is set somewhere between 20,000 and 40,000. Whatever the true figure, the German authorities simply could not cope with the dead. They used flame throwers on family shelters to incinerate the victims where they had died, or else piled up great stacks of bodies in the street - with sometimes as many as 500 bodies in them - and turned them into funeral pyres. Almost half of the homes in the city had been destroyed. Dresden would be attacked three more times by the 8th Air Force before the end of the war.

Just three weeks prior to the bombing of Dresden, Allied forces had liberated Auschwitz.

RUN FOR SHELTER

As February 1945 progressed into March, back in England people had started getting an inkling of just how terrible the Dresden raids had been. Churchill called for a review of bombing tactics admitting that *'The destruction of Dresden remains a serious query against the conduct of Allied bombing'*. His enthusiasm for helping the Soviets by targeting cities in their path had now notably waned and he was starting to feel somewhat magnanimous in anticipation of certain victory. Although the bombing of Dresden was not Harris's brainchild, he stoutly defended it on the grounds that it would help shorten the war. He lobbied for more, not less, bombing of German cities. An unfortunate press report declared that the Allies had decided to use the tactic of *'terror bombing'*. True or not, it could not help but have serious repercussions. Churchill had rebuked Harris for Dresden (and would do again after Bomber Command hit Potsdam). He had lost his taste for massed area bombing and instead, understanding that a German collapse was imminent, had set his thoughts on reconstruction. Harris took offence. He wrote to Churchill that:

'To suggest we have bombed German cities 'simply for the sake of increasing the terror though under other pretexts' and to speak of our offensive as including 'mere acts of wanton destruction' is both an insult to the bombing policy of the Air Ministry and to the manner in which that policy has been executed by Bomber Command.'

The note shows that Harris was no politician - and was getting further and further out on a very precarious limb...

TO THE BITTER END

The horrors of Dresden did not stop the bombing. On March 1, 478 Lancasters, Halifaxes and Mosquitoes attacked Mannheim in a brazen daylight raid. Within 24 hours, there were two more mass daylight raids, this time against Cologne. On 11 March, Bomber Command launched a 1,000 bomber raid on Essen - its largest daylight bomber operation of the entire war. Eighteen Mustang fighter squadrons flew escort as over 4,500 tons of bombs were deposited on what little remained of the city. As they withdrew, it was the turn of seven Spitfire squadrons to

BELOW: Churchill's crossing of the Rhine river in Germany, during Operation Plunder on 25 March 1945

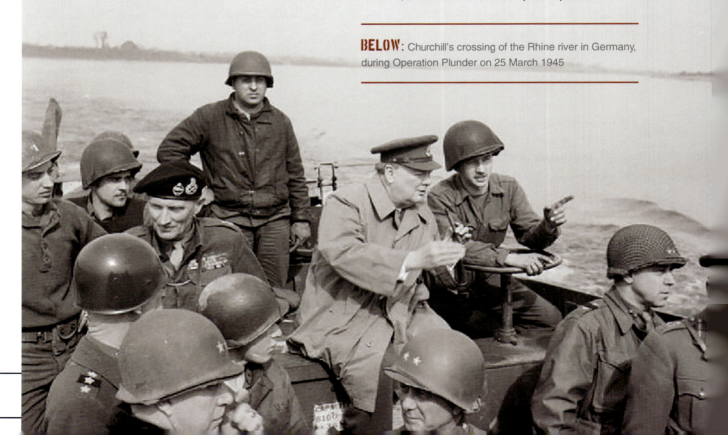

ABOVE: Ground crew of No 514 Squadron at Waterbeach load cement bags full of foodstuffs into the bomb bay of a Lancaster, 29 April 1945. The food would be dropped to the starving Dutch in those parts of Holland still occupied by the Germans, as part of Operation 'Manna'

escort them safely home. Only three Lancasters were lost in the raid. 16 March saw a bloody and protracted battle over Nuremberg which showed that German defences still had some teeth. 24 Lancasters were destroyed mostly by night fighters who had successfully infiltrated the 231 aircraft bomber stream during a night raid. March also saw three more raids on the burned-out city of Hamburg.

The end of March 1945 finally saw Allied troops crossing the Rhine into Germany and fighting their way east towards Soviet forces. They planned to link up at the River Elbe. In mid-April, over 100,000 German troops in the Ruhr surrendered before the Allies advance. Harris however, was far from convinced the war was either done or won. Mosquitoes were used incessantly to bomb Berlin until mid-April 1945, while a combined force of Lancasters and Mosquitoes attacked warships stuck in Kiel Harbour on 9 April. They sank the pocket battleship *Admiral Scheer* and effectively knocked out the *Admiral Hipper* and the *Emden*. Five days later, 599 Lancasters and Mosquitoes attacked the city of Potsdam with the aim of destroying the newly-relocated Luftwaffe HQ, military barracks and railway facilities, as well as the city centre. Churchill was not best pleased. *'What was the point..?'* he demanded

All attacks on Berlin did cease on 20 April but other raids continued. On 22 April, the port city of Bremen was *'softened up'* by 195 Lancasters before troops launched a ground operation. The port was in Allied hands by 26 April. The garrison of 6,000 troops there surrendered.

Everyone understood that these were the very last days, and the Heavies of Bomber Command were abruptly switched to humanitarian missions towards the end of April 1945. Starting on 26 April, Operation Exodus saw Bomber

'As we neared (Rotterdam) I took the big plane down so that we were just above the rooftops. Everywhere crowds of people were in the streets or at their windows, waving anything they could - handkerchiefs, flags and tablecloths - and every time I rocked the wings in return we could see them laughing and dancing with joy.... that afternoon I experienced the most emotional moment of my life.'

Flight Lieutenant H.G. Davies, 195 Squadron

Command aircraft flying out to Brussels and bringing home 999 British prisoners of war. By early June, that number had swelled to 75,000.

When famine broke out in Holland at the end of April, it was Lancasters from 1 and 3 Groups that brought them desperately needed supplies as part of *'Operation Manna'*. Instead of bombs now, they dropped food almost every single day, parachuting it down on Dutch airfields and racecourses from heights of just 500 feet. The Dutch people turned out in their masses to greet the bombers, waving British flags and cheering as they roared low overhead towards their drop zones. In total, 6,684 tons of needed food was dropped, with the Americans joining in and dropping still more supplies. To men used to pounding and burning enemy cities, it felt so good to help people now.

Bomber Command's last loss of the war came on 2 May over Kiel, when two Halifaxes collided in mid-air. Amazingly, three of their crew managed to survive. And then it was over. Bomber Command HQ at High Wycombe received a short message from the Air Ministry:

'All German land and sea and air forces will cease active operations at 0001/B hours on May 9.'

THE COOK'S TOUR

With hostilities over, bomber pilots started to fly some of their 'Erks over to Germany to see what it had all been about and to say thank you. It proved a mixed blessing. Seeing a city at night from 20,000 feet was very different to coming in at 500 feet in broad daylight and witnessing below nothing but scorched rubble and ash for miles and miles. What started off as a bit of a jolly with lots of bravado often descended into total stunned silence for the rest of the journey.

TIGER FORCE

As early as September 1944, the Allies had made detailed plans for after they had defeated Nazi Germany and could move on to the breaking of Imperial Japan. Churchill suggested at the Quebec Conference that a large part of RAF Bomber Command might be transferred out to the Pacific. It would be stationed on American bases on Okinawa and provide air support for an invasion of the rest of the Japanese islands. 40 squadrons of 'heavies' with a strong Commonwealth contingent would be despatched under the command of Air Marshal Sir Hugh Lloyd.

The nuclear strikes on Hiroshima and Nagasaki in August 1945 rendered all the preparations irrelevant. Tiger Force was officially disbanded on 31 October 1945.

LEFT: The first Quebec Conference, Canada. Group photograph on the terrace of the Citadel in Quebec. Front row: President Roosevelt of the United States and the Earl of Athlone, Governor General of Canada; back row: Mr Mackenzie-King, Prime Minister of Canada and the Prime Minister, the Right Hon Winston Churchill, MP

RIGHT: Air Vice Marshal Hugh Pughe Lloyd

1945 AND BEYOND

129

Bomber Command Commemorative Medal

Air Chief Marshal Sir Arthur T Harris, Commander in Chief of Royal Air Force Bomber Command, discussing an operation with the Senior Air Staff Officer, Air Vice Marshal R D Oxland, CB, CBE, and Mr M T Spence, OBE

Lancasters flew 156,000 sorties during the war. They dropped 608,612 tons of He and over 51 million incendiary devices. Just 24 aircraft survived 100 sorties. 8,325 aircraft were lost in action, 3,932 of them Lancasters (over half of the total number built).

Bomber Command sustained the highest loss rate of any major branch of the British armed forces during the Second World War. Out of the 125,000 men who served as aircrew, 55,573 were killed - a staggering fatality rate of 45%. (The Charge of the Light Brigade saw just 17% dead). Another 8,403 men sustained serious wounds and 9,838 were taken as prisoners of war. Bomber Command won a total of 19 Victoria Crosses during the war. Nine were posthumous.

Politicians were now turning their attention to building the peace. Few wanted to get smeared with the growing row over Bomber Command's strategy, and even fewer could grasp the difference between honouring the great sacrifice made by the men of the command, and the stark nationalistic jingoism which they once deliberately inflamed but which now did not suit their purposes anymore.

Harris was not given another job. He retired on 15 September 1946 and was brusquely pushed aside by the 'Men from the Ministry', who cared less about dead German civilians than they did the thought of further suffering this rum cove of a man whose face just didn't fit.

The men of Bomber Command were not issued their own campaign medal, unlike virtually everyone else in the British military. Harris took enormous umbrage and turned down accepting a peerage in 1946 in support of his men. By 1948, he had left the country for South Africa, having failed to find the necessary support to gain a British government post in Rhodesia. In 1953 he returned to England, where Churchill absolutely insisted that he accepted a Baronetcy. This time, Harris accepted. In 1985, Lady Jill Harris, his widow, with the aid of Air Vice Marshal D C T Bennett, launched an unofficial 'Bomber Command Commemorative Medal'. Sadly, although most definitely not a commercial venture, this had to be purchased at the cost of around £25, but still several thousand surviving veterans and their relatives purchased one. In 2013, the Ministry of Defence finally issued a clasp to all Bomber Command veterans which could be attached to the 1939 and 1945 Star medal. Many considered it an insult. 'Mine is still in the box, and there it will stay until we get a medal,' said 'Johnny' Johnson, the last surviving British Dambuster.

In August 2006, Lincoln Cathedral unveiled a monument to the men of Bomber Command and a further memorial was unveiled by Her Majesty Queen Elizabeth II on 28 June 2012 in London's Green Park. It has been vandalised on several occasions. In October 2015 a further memorial and Walls of Names were opened to the public in Lincoln at the International Bomber Command Centre.

Arthur Harris had a statue dedicated to him in 1992. Despite German protests, the Bomber Harris Trust (an RAF veterans' organisation set up to support Harris's reputation and memory) unveiled a statue of him in front of the RAF Church of St. Clement Danes, London. An inscription on the statue reads: 'The Nation owes them all an immense debt.' The Queen Mother unveiled the statue amidst screams of abuse from demonstrators. Like the memorial in Green Park, it has been vandalised a number of times and in 2021 there were attempts to have it torn down. Air Chief Marshal Sir Arthur Travers Harris is also remembered in the RAF chapel in Westminster Abbey.

SURVIVORS

With the end of the war, Bomber Command had little use for their old Lancasters and they only stayed on until the Lincoln was ready and available to replace them. A year after the war, some Lancasters of No 35 Squadron were sent on a publicity tour of the United States and were enthusiastically autographed by movie stars. Others made around the world flights or were despatched to the North Pole. In 1947 a relative few were stripped of their weaponry and converted for photoreconnaissance roles over Africa with No 82 Squadron and a few more were passed over to Coastal Command. A smattering of others were converted to civilian freighters and tankers.

The Argentine government bought 15 spare Lancasters in 1949, using them to put down civil insurrections in the country. In 1952, 59 Lancaster B.Is and B.VIIs were sent off to join the French Navy and served in search and rescue and reconnaissance roles until the 1960s. The RCAF too enthusiastically converted 70 of their Lancaster Mk.X's for use as maritime patrol aircraft and submarine hunters. More were converted for passenger use, flying a route from Montreal to Prestwick in Scotland.

In 1953, Bomber Command's final Lancaster was officially retired.

Many, many more were simply scrapped. The aircraft flown by Guy Gibson on the Dambusters raid was ignominiously put on the scrap heap at Wroughton as early as 1947. Most of the other surviving Dambusters aircraft met the same fate. In an austere post-war Britain, scrap metal had value; heroism not so much.

Today only 17 Lancasters survive in various states. Four of them actually saw service during WWII and only two can still fly. None were built by Avro. By far the greatest numbers of survivors were built by Victory Aircraft in Canada, which helps to explain why eight Lancasters can still be found there.

LEFT: RAF Bomber the Lancaster holds an "at home" party. Manchester folk, proud of the city's wonder-bomber, flocked to Piccadilly in their thousands when one of the machines was on a War Savings Campaign. August 1945

1945 AND BEYOND

135

SURVIVORS OF NOTE INCLUDE

R5868 - a static Lancaster now on display at the RAF Museum, Hendon. OL-Q 'Queen' is one of the four survivors who saw wartime service and is the oldest surviving Lancaster. It was delivered to No 83 Squadron in June 1942 and was transferred just over year later to the Australian 467 Squadron where it became PO-S 'Sugar'. It flew a quite incredible 137 combat missions.

W4783, which now serves at the Australian War Memorial in Canberra, also saw service, flying a total of 89 sorties with 460 Squadron as AR-G 'G - George'. Having been delivered in October 1942, it served in Britain until 1944, when it was flown to Brisbane to join the RAAF.

BELOW: W4783, G for George

OPP PAGE: R5868, during wartime

KB839 is on static display at the Greenwood Military Aviation Museum in Nova Scotia, Canada. During the war it flew a combined total of 26 sorties, first with 431 Squadron as SE 'G-George' and then with 419 Squadron as VR 'D-Daisy.'

KB882 is currently being restored with the intention of going on static display at the National Air Force Museum of Canada in 2024. This Lancaster was first given to 431 Squadron and then transferred to 428 Squadron, where it was designated NA 'R-Rabbit'. The Rabbit flew a total of 19 combat sorties.

NX611, better known to the world as 'Just Jane', currently resides at the Lincolnshire Aviation Heritage Centre in East Kirkby, Lincolnshire. Sold off after the war to the French Navy as a converted reconnaissance aircraft, it returned home in 1965. For over a decade, it served as the gate guardian of RAF Scampton, before being purchased by farming brothers Fred and Harold Panton in September 1983 with the intent of being fully restored. The work is still ongoing, but that which makes Just Jane so exciting is that all four of its Merlins work, and the bomber regularly makes taxi runs that can be viewed by the public. Taxi rides in the Lancaster are bookable. The aircraft was first purchased by the Pantons as a tribute to their older brother who died flying bombers during WWII.

FM213 was built in Toronto by Victory Aircraft and converted to a maritime reconnaissance variant for use by the Canadian Air Force in the early 1950s. After years on static display it was restored and flew again for the first time on 11 September 1988. It still flies today, one of only two airworthy Lancasters in the world. The aircraft is kept in the livery of KB726 of 419 'Moose' Squadron. This is to honour wartime hero Andrew Mynarski VC. Pilot officer Mynarski won his posthumous Victoria Cross aboard Lancaster KB726 on the night of 13 June 1944 trying to save his trapped rear gunner from an inferno.

PA474 'Spirit of Lincoln' still serves with the Battle of Britain Memorial Flight and is one of just two Lancasters still flying today. Built by Vickers-Armstrong in 1945, it was originally intended to serve in Tiger Force, it was instead converted for photoreconnaissance work over Africa. It joined the BoBMF in 1973, after being expertly restored at RAF Waddington. Its paint scheme is changed every so often so as to salute Lancasters of historical note.

MAIN IMAGE: PA474

OPP PAGE LEFT: KB882

OPP PAGE RIGHT: NX611

BELOW:
Prince William, Duke of Cambridge poses for a photograph with Battle of Britain veterans in front of a Lancaster bomber during a visit to The Battle Of Britain Memorial Flight to mark it's 60th anniversary at RAF Coningsby on July 11, 2017 in Coningsby, England

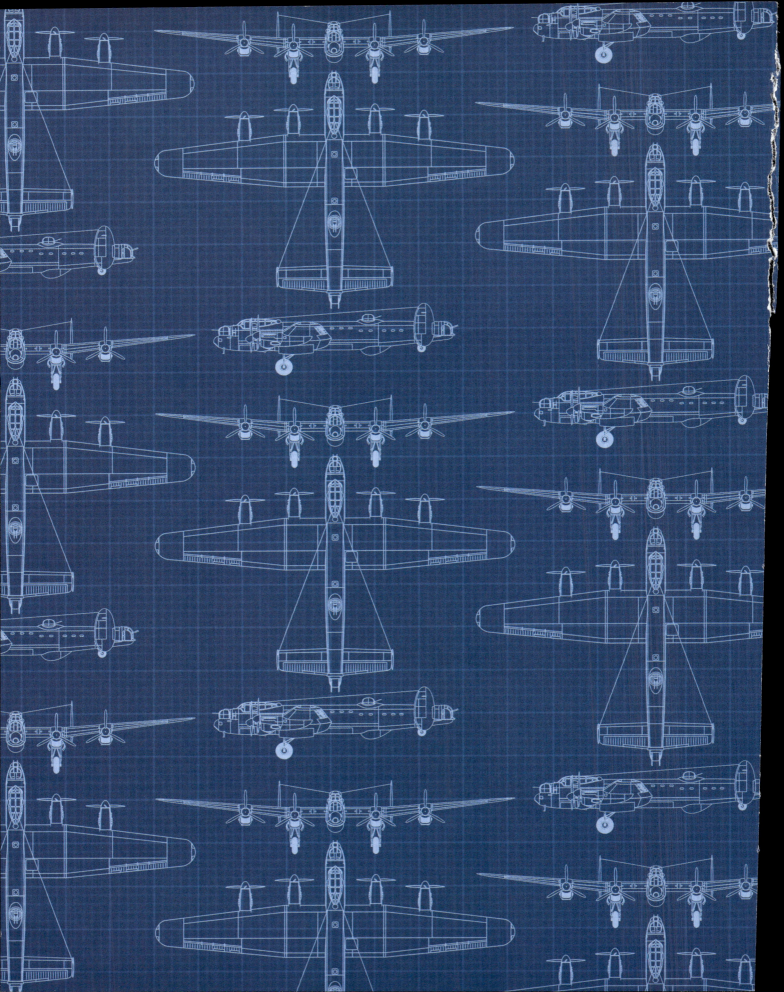